Super-Easy
Air Fryer

Cookbook with Pictures

Crisp & Delicious Air Fryer Recipes for Beginners | Easy-to-Follow
Instructions with Pictures to Make Home Cooking Easy

Jennifer Sotelo

Table of Contents

Introduction

Oil is known to be detrimental to our health, with research indicating that high fat intake can cause weight gain, heart disease, and cancer. Therefore, it's vital to monitor our oil usage in cooking and favor recipes that require minimal oil. Such recipes not only help cut down our fat consumption but also enhance the flavor and texture of dishes. They also tend to be quicker and easier to prepare, which is perfect for busy evenings.

Among various cooking methods, air fryers stand out as the healthiest option. They use little to no oil, which can reduce the fat content of food by up to 80% compared to traditional frying methods. Air fryers also cook food rapidly and evenly, preserving more nutrients and avoiding the creation of harmful substances like acrylamide. For those looking to lower calorie intake or avoid toxic chemicals, air fryers are an excellent choice.

Air fryers have become increasingly popular for their ability to cook food quickly using minimal or no oil. This method has made healthier alternatives to beloved fried foods like French fries, chicken wings, and mozzarella sticks. Food cooked in an air fryer is not only healthier but also tends to be more flavorful and crispier. This is because air fryers use significantly less oil, which allows the natural flavors of the food to stand out. Furthermore, the higher cooking temperatures in air fryers help achieve a crispier exterior, making air fryer dishes preferable for both taste and health.

The Fundamentals of an Air Fryer

What Is an Air Fryer?

An air fryer is a handy kitchen appliance that cook food by circulating hot air around it, using a fan to achieve a crispy, fried-like texture. These devices are typically compact, making them easy to store on a countertop or inside a cabinet. Most air fryers come equipped with a basket or tray for the food, a timer to specify cooking duration, and often include temperature controls for precise cooking. Air fryers allow for cooking with minimal or no oil, which significantly cuts down on fat and calories in your meals. They also ensure food is cooked quickly and uniformly, helping you avoid undercooked or overcooked dishes.

Unlike conventional frying, air fryers require little to no oil, reducing not only the fat content in meals but also the potential formation of harmful carcinogens. Moreover, air fryers cook food faster than traditional methods, offering a practical solution for time-pressed households. They are highly versatile, capable of preparing everything from snacks to full meals effortlessly. Given these benefits, it's clear why air fryers are becoming an essential fixture in kitchens nationwide.

Understanding the Components of an Air Fryer

To fully grasp how air fryers work, it's important to know the various parts and their functions:

Heating Element: Typically located at the top, the heating element generates the heat that warms the air inside the cooking chamber.

Fan: This component is responsible for distributing the hot air evenly around the food, ensuring uniform cooking on all sides.

Cooking Chamber: The main area where the food is cooked, the enclosed cooking chamber circulates hot air around the food to cook it thoroughly.

Cooking Tray or Basket: This is where the food to be fried is placed. It usually has a nonstick coating to prevent food from sticking and to facilitate easy cleaning.

Drip Tray: Positioned below the cooking basket or tray, the drip tray catches any excess oil or grease that falls off the food during cooking. This helps prevent smoke and splattering and keeps the appliance clean.

Control Panel: Here, you set the cooking temperature and time. Control panels may feature analog knobs or a digital interface, depending on the model.

Safety Features: Many air fryers include safety features such as automatic shut-off when the cooking basket is removed or once the cooking cycle ends.

Air fryers have become essential in modern kitchens for those seeking a healthier alternative to traditional frying methods. With their cutting-edge technology, variety of models, and thoughtfully designed components, air fryers continue to be a favorite choice. As long as there is demand for health-conscious cooking without compromising on flavor and texture, air fryers will remain a catalyst for culinary innovation and promote healthier eating habits.

Different Models of Air Fryer

To cater to diverse consumer preferences, air fryers come in a range of sizes and styles. Here's a look at some common types of air fryer models:

Basket Style Air Fryers: These are the traditional models of air fryers, featuring a removable basket that slides in and out of the cooking chamber. Available in various sizes, these models are ideal for individuals as well as families.

Oven-Style Air Fryers: Resembling countertop convection ovens, these air fryers offer expanded cooking capacity and versatility. They often include multiple racks, enabling you to bake, roast, and cook different dishes at the same time.

Toaster Oven/Air Fryer Combos: Combining functionalities, some air fryers integrate with toaster ovens. These units can toast, bake, broil, and air fry, optimizing countertop space while providing various cooking options.

Digital VS. Analog Controls: Air fryer controls can be digital or analog. Analog models are straightforward and user-friendly, whereas digital ones offer more precise control and typically feature preset programs for common dishes.

Step-By-Step Using Your Air Fryer

Getting accustomed to your air fryer might seem overwhelming at first, but with a little practice, you'll soon be making tasty, crispy dishes effortlessly. Here's how to master air frying:

Prepare the Air Fryer Basket

Before you begin, it's crucial to grease the basket or pan of your air fryer with cooking spray to prevent food from sticking and simplify cleanup. Lightly coat the inside of the basket or pan, including the sides and bottom. After cooking, cleaning up is as simple as wiping down the basket or pan with a paper towel or cloth.

Adjust the Temperature

Most air fryers come with a preheat option. Use this to preheat your air fryer for 5 minutes before adding your food. If yours doesn't have this feature, manually set the temperature and wait for 5 minutes. Remember, different foods will need various temperatures and times to cook properly. It's key to monitor your food and adjust the settings as needed for optimal results.

Preheat the Air Fryer

To preheat, set your air fryer to the desired temperature and let it run empty for a few minutes. This ensures even cooking and flavor retention.

Arrange Food in the Air Fryer

Once preheated, place your food in the basket. Ensure space between items for better airflow. This method works for a range of foods, from meats and vegetables to batter-based items like omelets and cakes.

Set the Cooking Time

Insert the basket and set the cooking time according to your recipe or package instructions. Make sure the basket is correctly positioned to ensure even cooking. If unsure, it's better to start with a shorter time and add more as needed.

Start Cooking

Press the start button to begin the cooking process. Most air fryers show an indicator light when they're active. Some models feature a pause button to stop cooking temporarily if you need to check on the food or make adjustments.

Flip the Food

For even cooking, flip your food occasionally, especially thicker cuts or larger pieces. Follow your recipe's guidance on when to flip—for instance, if it instructs a total cook time of 10 minutes, flip the food at the halfway point.

Finish and Serve

When the cooking time is up, remove the food from the air fryer. Always use oven mitts or gloves as the food and the air fryer will be hot. If not serving immediately, let the food cool on a plate or cutting board before serving or cutting into pieces.

Following these steps will help you get the most out of your air frying experience, turning you into an air fry pro in no time!

Benefits of Using It

The air fryer has become a significant culinary breakthrough in recent years. This innovative kitchen appliance offers numerous benefits, including time-efficient and healthier cooking options. As more families adopt it, understanding the advantages it brings is crucial.

Healthy Cooking:

Using an air fryer allows you to make excellent, crispy food with much less oil than using a conventional frying method. This is one of the most notable advantages of utilizing an air fryer. Traditionally, deep frying involves submerging food in heated oil producing heavy dishes with harmful fats. In contrast, the air fryer uses little to no oil. The mechanism of the air fryer uses hot air circulation to cook food, producing a crispy coating without using a lot of oil. For those concerned about their health, this amounts to fewer calories consumed and a lower risk of heart-related problems without sacrificing flavor or texture.

Versatile Cooking Options:

A wide variety of foods, including appetizers, main courses, and desserts, can be prepared using air fryers, which are highly adaptable.

The air fryer can cook everything, including baked delicacies like muffins and pastries, roasted veggies, and crispy chicken wings. The pre-programmed cooking settings for popular dishes that many air fryers have made it simple for anyone with no cooking expertise to make restaurant-quality meals at home. Thanks to its versatility, you may experiment with a range of recipes and cuisines, which promotes culinary discovery and creativity.

Retains Nutritional Value:

Beyond only using less oil, air frying keeps food's nutritional content better than conventional frying techniques. The food cooks rapidly and evenly with little loss of vitamins and minerals because of the hot air's rapid circulation. For instance, vegetables maintain brilliant colors, and meats are juicy and tender. Additionally, because air frying cooks food faster, nutrients have less time to degrade, making the food healthier and more nutrient-dense for you and your family.

Faster Cooking Time:

In today's hectic world, time is a valuable resource, and the air fryer shines at providing quick and effective cooking. Compared to conventional ovens, it can cook food up to 25% faster because of its quick air circulation and excellent temperature control. This makes it the perfect gadget for busy people and families because it allows you to enjoy a homemade, crispy supper in less time.

Easy Cleaning:

Even while cleanup after cooking might be tedious, the air fryer makes it easier. The removable nonstick cooking basket or tray found on the majority of air fryers is simple to wash by hand or in the dishwasher. Your kitchen's mess is further diminished by the absence of splattering oil and grease, making meal preparation and cleanup simple.

Energy Efficiency:

In comparison to conventional ovens, air fryers use less energy. They take less time to heat up and use less energy to maintain the proper temperature, thanks to their smaller cooking chambers. Your utility costs will eventually go down because of this efficiency, which also saves energy.

Safe and User Friendly:

There are safety features built into air fryers that make cooking worry-free. When the cooking cycle is finished, the majority of models have a built-in switch that shuts the appliance off. This prevents overcooking and lowers the chance of culinary mishaps. Additionally, air fryers are safer to operate than traditional deep fryers because of their small size and cool-touch exteriors. Traditional deep fryers can be dangerous to use because of their open design and heated oil.

Minimal Food Splattering:

Due to hot oil splattering, traditional frying techniques can result in filthy countertops and stovetops. This problem is resolved by air frying since no mess or splattering occurs because the food is contained in a sealed chamber. For those who detest the cleanliness required for frying, this feature makes air frying more tempting.

Customizable Cooking:

With the precise temperature and time settings provided by air fryers, you may cook according to your tastes. You can modify settings to suit your preferences, whether you like your fries extremely crispy or your chicken a little less browned. You can always expect your meals to be prepared exactly how you like them because of this level of customization.

Must-Have Accessories of Air Fryer

Enhancing your air frying experience can be as simple as equipping yourself with some essential accessories. These add-ons not only simplify the cooking process but also expand the range of dishes you can prepare. Here are some must-have accessories for any air fryer enthusiast:

1. Silicone Basket Liners
These reusable liners are a great alternative to parchment paper or aluminum foil. Made from food-grade silicone, they prevent food from sticking to the basket while ensuring proper air circulation for even cooking. They're easy to clean, dishwasher safe, and environmentally friendly due to their reusability.

2. Air Fryer Rack with Skewers
Maximize your air fryer's space and cooking capabilities with a multi-layered rack that includes skewers. This accessory is perfect for making kebabs, grilling vegetables, or cooking multiple food items simultaneously, allowing you to make full use of the vertical space within your air fryer. The stainless steel construction ensures durability and easy cleaning.

3. Oil Sprayer
An oil sprayer is an indispensable tool for those who want to use minimal oil but still achieve a crispy finish. Fill it with your oil of choice and use it to spray a fine mist over your food before cooking. This provides an even coat, better than drizzling and healthier than traditional frying methods.

4. Heat Resistant Tongs
When you're cooking at high temperatures, a pair of heat-resistant tongs can be a lifesaver. They allow you to easily handle and turn food items mid-cook without the risk of burns. Look for tongs with silicone tips to prevent scratching your air fryer's non-stick coating.

5. Baking Dish

A compatible baking dish or pan can transform your air fryer into a mini oven for baking cakes, bread, or quiches. Non-stick and the right size to fit inside your air fryer, these dishes make it easy to bake your favorites without turning on the oven, saving energy and keeping your kitchen cooler.

6. Temperature Probe

To ensure your meats and other dishes are cooked safely and to perfection, a temperature probe is crucial. This tool eliminates guesswork by letting you monitor the internal temperature of your food, ensuring it is perfectly cooked every time.

Investing in these accessories will not only enhance the functionality of your air fryer but also help you to explore new culinary possibilities, making every meal a little easier and a lot tastier. Whether you're a novice or a seasoned air fryer user, these tools are sure to make your experience more enjoyable and versatile.

Cleaning and Caring for Your Air Fryer

To ensure optimal performance and longevity, it's crucial to regularly clean and maintain your air fryer. Proper care not only keeps the appliance in excellent condition but also prolongs the life of its components. Here's a comprehensive guide to cleaning and maintaining your air fryer:

Disconnect and Cool Down: Always unplug the air fryer from the power source before cleaning. Allow it to cool completely to avoid burns or other accidents.

Clean Removable Parts: Most air fryers have parts that are dishwasher safe. Remove any parts that were used during cooking. You can clean these parts in the dishwasher or by hand using mild soap and warm water. Use a soft sponge or cloth to avoid scratching any non-stick surfaces.

Interior Cleaning: Wipe the inside of the air fryer with a damp cloth or sponge. Be careful to avoid abrasive cleaners or tools that could scratch the non-stick coating.

Tackle Tough Stains: For stubborn food particles or stains, make a paste of baking soda and water. Apply this paste to the affected areas and let it sit for a few minutes. Then, gently scrub with a soft brush or cloth and rinse well.

Clean the Heating Element: The heating element is crucial for your air fryer's operation. Use a soft brush or compressed air to remove any debris or food particles that may have accumulated around the heating element. Ensure it is completely clean to maintain efficient cooking.

Exterior Cleaning: Wipe the outside of the air fryer with a damp cloth or sponge. Take care not to let water seep into the control panel or openings to avoid damaging electrical components.

Proper Storage: When not in use, store your air fryer in a clean, dry place. Ensure the cord is neatly coiled and protected from damage.

Avoid Aerosol Cooking Sprays: Do not use aerosol cooking sprays as they can leave a difficult-to-remove residue. Instead, use a pastry brush or a small amount of oil applied with a brush for coating your food.

Routine Maintenance: Regularly check for any loose screws or components that may need tightening. Consult the owner's

manual for troubleshooting tips, or contact customer support if you encounter any performance issues with your air fryer.

By following these cleaning and maintenance tips, you can keep your air fryer in prime condition, ensuring it continues to produce delicious and healthy meals with ease.

Frequently Asked Questions

Air fryers have gained a lot of popularity as a kitchen appliance because they require very little oil to make crispy and flavorful meals. However, many people still have questions about the benefits of air fryers and how to use them effectively. Here are some frequently asked questions about air fryers:

What is an air fryer, and how does it work?

An air fryer is a kitchen appliance that cooks by circulating hot air around the food using a heating element and a fan. This rapid air movement cooks the food quickly and evenly, achieving a crispy texture similar to traditional frying but with significantly less oil.

Can you cook frozen foods in an air fryer?

Yes, air fryers are excellent for cooking frozen foods like fish sticks, chicken wings, and French fries directly from the freezer. Adjust the cooking time as necessary according to your air fryer's guidelines.

What types of foods can I cook in an air fryer?

You can prepare a wide range of foods in an air fryer, including:

Frozen items such as fries and mozzarella sticks.

Fresh or marinated proteins like salmon fillets, steaks, and chicken wings.

Vegetables such as Brussels sprouts, broccoli, and zucchini.

Baked goods like cookies, cakes, and muffins.

Reheat leftovers to restore their crispy texture.

Do I need to use oil in an air fryer?

Adding a small amount of oil, such as a spritz or a few drops brushed on, can enhance the flavor and crispiness of some foods. However, many recipes and food items can be cooked without any oil at all.

Can I use aluminum foil in the air fryer basket or tray?

Yes, aluminum foil can be used in the air fryer basket or tray with precautions:

Ensure the foil does not block airflow by completely covering the basket or tray.

Leave some space around the edges for air to circulate freely.

Consider using perforated foil to prevent moisture buildup.

Can I shake or flip the food in the middle of cooking?
It is advisable to shake or turn the food halfway through the cooking process to ensure even frying and a consistent crispy texture.

Are air fryers energy-efficient?
Air fryers are generally more energy-efficient than conventional ovens because they heat up and cook food faster. However, energy efficiency can vary by brand and model.

Do I need to preheat my air fryer?
Preheating your air fryer can help achieve more even cooking, though it's not always necessary. Preheat for a few minutes to the desired temperature for best results.

Can I use my air fryer for reheating leftovers?
Reheating leftovers in an air fryer is excellent for restoring the crispiness and flavor of foods like pizza, fries, and chicken as if they were freshly made.

Are there any foods that are not suitable for cooking in an air fryer?
While air fryers are versatile, some foods might not perform well, such as those needing immersion in a deep fryer or items with high moisture content that are heavily battered.

Can I use store-bought frozen foods in the air fryer?
Yes, store-bought frozen foods like chicken nuggets and spring rolls can be cooked in an air fryer. Follow the package's recommended cooking times and temperatures, adjusting as needed for your appliance.

How do I prevent my air fryer from smoking?
To minimize smoke, keep your air fryer clean and free of grease and food debris. Avoid overcrowding the basket, and consider using foil or a drip tray to catch excess fat when cooking high-fat items.

4-Week Meal Plan

Week 1

Day 1:
Breakfast: Mini Ham Quiches
Lunch: Cheese Bacon Loaded Potato Boats
Snack: Cheese Jalapeño Poppers
Dinner: Garlic Chicken Meatballs
Dessert: Homemade Leches Cake

Day 2:
Breakfast: Classic Quiche Lorraine
Lunch: Lemony Brussels Sprouts with Sun-Dried Tomatoes
Snack: Delicious Beef Taquitos
Dinner: Lemon-Garlic Shrimp
Dessert: Cinnamon Apple Chips

Day 3:
Breakfast: Lemon Rosemary Scones
Lunch: Air Fried Corn with Cheese
Snack: Crispy Chicken Spring Rolls
Dinner: Aromatic Tomato Beef Casserole
Dessert: Tasty Oat-Berries Crisp

Day 4:
Breakfast: Mini Bacon Quiche Pie
Lunch: Yogurt-Flavored Sweet Potato Wedges
Snack: Dehydrated Gingered Orange Slices
Dinner: Beer Roasted Chicken Thighs
Dessert: Flavorful Cinnamon Pecan Pie

Day 5:
Breakfast: Homemade Pancakes
Lunch: Easy Dehydrated Plum Tomatoes
Snack: Bacon Wrapped Asparagus
Dinner: Breaded Fish Fillets
Dessert: Typical Cinnamon Churros

Day 6:
Breakfast: Cheese Cornbread
Lunch: Air Fried Paprika Cauliflower
Snack: Granola Almond Blueberries Mix
Dinner: Cheese Beef Meatballs
Dessert: Homemade Streusel Cake

Day 7:
Breakfast: Cheese Sausage and Egg Burritos
Lunch: Breaded Parmesan Green Beans
Snack: Spiced Pumpkin Strips with Yogurt Sauce
Dinner: Orange-Flavored Duck Breasts
Dessert: Air Fried Pecan Pie

Week 2

Day 1:
Breakfast: Tasty Cheddar Scallion Biscuits
Lunch: Italian Seasoned Zucchini Sticks
Snack: Savory Beef Meatballs
Dinner: Turkey-Mushroom Patties
Dessert: Vanilla Blueberry Pie

Day 2:
Breakfast: Blueberry Granola Bowl
Lunch: Breaded Garlicky Brussels Sprouts
Snack: Cheese Bacon Stuffed Jalapeño Peppers
Dinner: Beer Broiled White Fish Fillets
Dessert: Fluffy Cinnamon Cakes

Day 3:
Breakfast: Banana Pecan Bread
Lunch: Crispy Kale Chips
Snack: Crispy Avocado Slices
Dinner: Fried Rosemary-Garlic Veal Loin
Dessert: The Best Blueberry Pie

Day 4:
Breakfast: Air Fried French Toast
Lunch: Cheese Broccoli Stuffed Mushrooms
Snack: Crunchy Onion Rings
Dinner: Peach-Flavored Chicken Wings
Dessert: Cinnamon Peaches

Day 5:
Breakfast: Easy Scrambled Eggs
Lunch: Air-Fried Lemon Garlic Broccoli
Snack: Cheddar Jalapeño Cornbread
Dinner: Savory Tuna Burgers
Dessert: Apple Dumplings

Day 6:
Breakfast: Easy Mac & Cheese Casserole
Lunch: Honey-Roasted Parsnips with Cheese Dip
Snack: Crunchy Spicy Chickpeas
Dinner: Pork Chop & Mashed Potato Casserole
Dessert: Strawberry Oats Crumble

Day 7:
Breakfast: Cheesy Spinach-Tomato Frittata
Lunch: Cheese Spinach-Zucchini Casserole
Snack: Mini Cheese Sausage Pizzas
Dinner: BBQ Chicken Drumsticks
Dessert: Baked Walnut Pie

Week 3

Day 1:
Breakfast: Avocado Egg Boats
Lunch: Herbed Zucchini Slices & Bell Peppers
Snack: Roasted Cheese Potato Skins
Dinner: Palatable Korean-Style Fried Chicken Thighs
Dessert: The Best Blueberry Pie

Day 2:
Breakfast: Chive-Cream Cheese Omelet
Lunch: Roasted Brussels Sprouts with Parmesan Cheese
Snack: Simple Fried Plantain Pieces
Dinner: Crunchy Popcorn Shrimp
Dessert: Cream Cheese Chocolate Mug Cake

Day 3:
Breakfast: Garlic Cheese-Broccoli Soufflés
Lunch: Cheese-Herb Stuffed Tomato Halves
Snack: Delicious Beef Taquitos
Dinner: Roasted Garlic Lamb Leg
Dessert: Tasty Oat-Berries Crisp

Day 4:
Breakfast: Cinnamon Banana Bread Pudding
Lunch: Herb-Garlic Carrots & Turnips
Snack: Cheese Jalapeño Poppers
Dinner: Aromatic Szechuan Chicken Wings
Dessert: Typical Cinnamon Churros

Day 5:
Breakfast: Flavorful Vanilla French Toast
Lunch: Cheese Broccoli Casserole
Snack: Crispy Chicken Spring Rolls
Dinner: Garlic Roasted Lobster Tails
Dessert: Cinnamon Peaches

Day 6:
Breakfast: Apple French Toast
Lunch: Buttered Acorn Squash Slices
Snack: Dehydrated Gingered Orange Slices
Dinner: Buttered Garlicky Steaks
Dessert: Hazelnuts Orange Cake

Day 7:
Breakfast: Vanilla Pecan Granola
Lunch: Lemony Brussels Sprouts with Sun-Dried Tomatoes
Snack: Bacon Wrapped Asparagus
Dinner: Yogurt-Marinated Chicken Drumsticks
Dessert: Cinnamon Apple Chips

Week 4

Day 1:
Breakfast: Classic Quiche Lorraine
Lunch: Cheese Bacon Loaded Potato Boats
Snack: Granola Almond Blueberries Mix
Dinner: Herb-Butter Roasted Turkey Breast
Dessert: Fluffy Cinnamon Cakes

Day 2:
Breakfast: Cheese Spinach & Cherry Tomato Frittata
Lunch: Breaded Garlicky Brussels Sprouts
Snack: Spiced Pumpkin Strips with Yogurt Sauce
Dinner: Homemade Bacon Wrapped Scallops
Dessert: Air Fried Pecan Pie

Day 3:
Breakfast: Mini Ham Quiches
Lunch: Air Fried Corn with Cheese
Snack: Savory Beef Meatballs
Dinner: Roasted Tomahawk Steaks
Dessert: Soft Chocolate Lava Cakes

Day 4:
Breakfast: Lemon Rosemary Scones
Lunch: Yogurt-Flavored Sweet Potato Wedges
Snack: Crispy Avocado Slices
Dinner: Simple Baked Cornish Hen
Dessert: Flavorful Cinnamon Pecan Pie

Day 5:
Breakfast: Mini Bacon Quiche Pie
Lunch: Easy Dehydrated Plum Tomatoes
Snack: Cheese Bacon Stuffed Jalapeño Peppers
Dinner: Flavorful Tuna Arugula Salad
Dessert: Baked Walnut Pie

Day 6:
Breakfast: Homemade Pancakes
Lunch: Air Fried Paprika Cauliflower
Snack: Crunchy Onion Rings
Dinner: Cajun Croutons-Crusted Pork Chops
Dessert: Cinnamon Apple Chips

Day 7:
Breakfast: Cheese Cornbread
Lunch: Breaded Parmesan Green Beans
Snack: Cheddar Jalapeño Cornbread
Dinner: Delicious Sardine-Zucchini Patties
Dessert: Homemade Coco Almond Cake

Chapter 1 Breakfast Recipes

Mini Bacon Quiche Pie

⏰ Prep: 15 minutes   🍲 Cook: 20 minutes   🍽 Serves: 6

6 ounces cream cheese, softened
5 teaspoons 2% milk
2 large eggs, room temperature
½ cup Colby cheese, shredded
2 tablespoons green pepper, chopped

1 tablespoon onion, finely chopped
1 tube (8-ounces) refrigerated crescent rolls
5 bacon strips, cooked and crumbled
Green onions, thinly sliced (optional)

1. Preheat the air fryer at 325°F/165°C. 2. Whisk the cream cheese and milk to a smooth liquid in a bowl. Then beat the eggs and add cheese, onion, and chopped green pepper. 3. Prepare 6 muffin cups and divide the crescent rolls into the cups, pressing onto the sides of the muffin cups. 4. Sprinkle half of the cooked bacon into the cups. Drizzle the egg mixture over the bacon and sprinkle the remaining bacon on top. 5. Arrange the muffin cups onto the baking tray in the air fryer. 6. Bake them in the preheated air fryer for 20 minutes. 7. When cooked, insert a tester in the tarts and the tester should come out clean with the muffins getting browned lightly around the edges. 8. Repeat the steps with the remaining muffins. 9. Serve and enjoy!

Per Serving: Calories 192; Fat 14.89g; Sodium 313mg; Carbs 6.95g; Fiber 0.5g; Sugar 2.61g; Protein 8.31g

Homemade Pancakes

⏰ Prep: 15 minutes   🍲 Cook: 10 minutes   🍽 Serves: 4

1½ cups flour
3½ teaspoons baking powder
1½ teaspoons baking soda
1 teaspoon salt

1 tablespoon sugar
1¼ cups milk
1 egg
3 tablespoons melted butter

1. Preheat the air fryer at 220°F/105°C on Bake mode. 2. Add all the ingredients to a large blender, and blend them well, then let the mixture rest for 4 minutes. 3. Spritz the suitable baking pan with non-stick cooking spray. Evenly arrange the mixture on the pan, as thin as possible. 4. Bake the food for 6 minutes until golden. 5. Carefully remove from the air fryer when the time is up. 6. Serve and enjoy!

Per Serving: Calories 3; Fat 12.65g; Sodium 1175mg; Carbs 43.55g; Fiber 1.4g; Sugar 5.98g; Protein 8.72g

Cheese Cornbread

⏰ Prep: 10 minutes   🍲 Cook: 60 minutes   🍽 Serves: 10

1 box corn muffin mix
½ cup butter, melted
1 can whole kernel corn, drained
1 can cream-style corn

1 cup sour cream
2 eggs
8 ounces cheddar cheese, shredded

1. Brush the inside of a casserole dish with butter, then crack in the eggs and beat them. Let the mixture sit. 2. Add the melted butter to the dish, and then add the corn. 3. Mix in the eggs and sour cream. 4. Add half the cheese and stir well to combine. 5. Stir in the muffin mix until blended. Add the remaining cheese on top. 6. Bake the food in the air fryer at 375°F/190°C for 60 minutes until the center is just fluffy.7. Serve and enjoy!

Per Serving: Calories 267; Fat 16.55g; Sodium 524mg; Carbs 24.32g; Fiber 1.6g; Sugar 3.48g; Protein 7.63g

Classic Quiche Lorraine

⏰ Prep: 15 minutes   🍳 Cook: 40 minutes   🍽 Serves: 4

Quiche crust (choose one)
1 homemade quiche crust   1 prepared pie shell, fridge, or frozen
Bacon filling
1 tablespoon butter   ½ onion, finely chopped
1 garlic clove, minced   3 ounces bacon, cut into small strips
Egg mixture
4 eggs   Cheese
1¼ cup heavy cream   1¼ cup grated Gruyère cheese
Pinch of salt and pepper

1. Cook the quiche crust or the prepared pie shell according to the package instruction, and then transfer to a quiche tin. 2. In a skillet, Melt the butter in a skillet over medium-high heat; add the bacon strips, minced garlic, and chopped onion and cook them until the bacon is lightly golden. When cooked, transfer to a bowl lined with paper. Set it aside to cool. 3. Beat the eggs with heavy cream, salt, and pepper in a bowl. 4. Place the quiche tin on the cooking tray and insert it together inside the air fryer. 5. Sprinkle the bacon mixture evenly across the cooked quiche crust. 6. Drizzle the cream mixture evenly on top. 7. Push some of the cream mixture or the bacon below the surface. 8. Bake them in the air fryer at 390°F/200°C for 35 to 40 minutes or until the top is golden and the center is still jiggle. 9. When cooked, garnish the dish with some extra bacon as you like. 10. Allow it to rest for 10 minutes. Then carefully remove it from the air fryer. 11. Serve and enjoy!

Per Serving: Calories 663; Fat 51.54g; Sodium 1263mg; Carbs 31.08g; Fiber 1.8g; Sugar 2.7g; Protein 20.73g

Mini Ham Quiches

⏰ Prep: 5 minutes   🍳 Cook: 20 minutes   🍽 Serves: 12

1 cup salad croutons   1½ teaspoons dried parsley flakes
1 cup cheddar cheese, shredded   ½ teaspoon Dijon mustard
1 cup fully cooked ham, chopped   ¼ teaspoon salt
4 large eggs   ⅛ teaspoon onion powder
1½ cups 2% milk   Dash of pepper

1. Preheat the air fryer at 325°F/160°C on Bake mode. 2. Prepare a 12-cup muffin pan and divide the croutons, cheese, and ham in the muffin cups. 3. Beat eggs with milk, parsley flakes, Dijon mustard, salt, onion powder, and pepper in a large bowl until well mixed. 4. Divide the egg mixture in the muffin cups. 5. Bake the food for 20 minutes; when done, a tester should be clean after being inserted out from the quiche, and the edges should be lightly browned.5.Serve and enjoy!

Per Serving: Calories 209; Fat 19.11g; Sodium 426mg; Carbs 2.91g; Fiber 0g; Sugar 2.38g; Protein 6.05g

Lemon Rosemary Scones

⏰ Prep: 5 minutes   🍳 Cook: 15 minutes   🍽 Serves: 2

1½ cups all-purpose flour   ¼ cup plus 2 tablespoons unsalted butter, cold,
2 teaspoons sugar   and cut into pieces
1½ teaspoons baking powder   ½ cup plus 2 tablespoons well-shaken
¼ teaspoon baking soda   buttermilk, divided
½ teaspoon salt   Butter, softened, for serving (optional)
⅛ teaspoon freshly ground black pepper   Lemon curd for serving (optional)
½ teaspoon lemon zest, finely grated   Clotted cream for serving (optional)
1½ teaspoons fresh rosemary, finely chopped

1. Sift the sugar, baking powder, salt, baking soda, black pepper, and flour in a medium bowl; add rosemary and lemon zest and use a fork to combine. 2. Blend the mixture into a coarse crumb, and then add the butter into the flour with a fork. 3. Stir in ½ cup plus 1 tablespoon of the buttermilk with a fork, and the mixture should be just moistened. 4. Press the dough and form it into a rough ball. 5. Lightly dust a clean work surface and your hands. Pat the dough and then continue to knead until it just comes together. Shape into a rectangle. 6. Then roll the dough into ¾-inch thick with a lightly floured rolling pin. 7. Cut the dough crosswise into 3 portions and then cut each into 2 triangle-shaped scones. 8. Evenly arrange the scones on the baking pan, and brush them with the remaining buttermilk. 9. Place the baking pan in the air fryer, and Bake them at 400°F/200°C for 14 minutes. 10. When cooked, carefully remove it from the air fryer. 11. Serve with lemon curd, clotted cream, jam, or butter. Enjoy!

Per Serving: Calories 530; Fat 17.63g; Sodium 825mg; Carbs 79.37g; Fiber 2.7g; Sugar 5.98g; Protein 13.17g

Cheese Sausage and Egg Burritos

⏰ Prep: 15 minutes   🍲 Cook: 25 minutes   🍽 Serves: 6

1-pound ground breakfast sausage
8 eggs
¼ cup milk
Kosher salt
Pepper

1 tablespoon butter
6 large burrito-size tortillas
2 cups shredded cheese of choice
6 tablespoons maple syrup
Olive oil cooking spray

1. Cook the ground sausage in the skillet over medium heat for 6 to 8 minutes, breaking them up halfway through cooking. When cooked, transfer to a plate. 2. Beat the eggs with milk, pepper, and kosher salt for about 1 minute in a mixing bowl.3. Melt the butter in a pan over medium-low heat; add the egg mixture and cook them for 4 to 5 minutes until the eggs are cooked and scrambled. 4. Prepare the cheese, tortillas, cooked sausage, maple syrup, and scrambled eggs. 5. In the center of each burrito, add some cheddar, sausage, scrambled eggs, and 1 tablespoon of maple syrup, and then fold them in. Fold the top over the filling. 6. Arrange evenly 2 to 3 burritos onto the baking tray, and spray olive oil cooking spray over both sides. 7. Air fry the burritos in the air fryer at 325°F/165°C for 10 minutes. 6.When cooked, carefully remove it from the air fryer. Serve and enjoy!

Per Serving: Calories 642; Fat 37.66g; Sodium 1212mg; Carbs 40.57g; Fiber 1.3g; Sugar 15g; Protein 34.02g

Blueberry Granola Bowl

⏰ Prep: 5 minutes   🍲 Cook: 40 minutes   🍽 Serves: 4

For the dehydrated blueberries
4 cups blueberries, rinsed
For the granola
2 cups oats
½ cup sunflower seeds, walnuts, and almonds
½ cup brown sugar
1 teaspoon cinnamon

1 teaspoon nutmeg
4 tablespoons wheat germ
6 tablespoons butter, melted
1 tablespoon vanilla extract

To prepare the blueberries: 1. Evenly arrange the blueberries on the cooking tray. 2. Set the air fryer to Dehydrate function, and adjust the temperature to 120°F/50°C and time to 20 hours. 3. Press Start/Stop to begin cooking.
To prepare the granola: 1. Mix all the granola ingredients in a bowl, then evenly spread the mixture on the baking pan. 2. Bake the granola mixture at 300°F/150°C for 30 minutes, stirring them halfway through. 3. When the granola has cooked, carefully remove it from the air fryer. 4. Mix the granola with the dried blueberries, and you can serve with yogurt.

Per Serving: Calories 599; Fat 30.98g; Sodium 151mg; Carbs 87.99g; Fiber 13.7g; Sugar 43.02g; Protein 14.8g

Tasty Cheddar Scallion Biscuits

⏰ Prep: 15 minutes   🍲 Cook: 10 minutes   🍽 Serves: 6

1¼ cup all-purpose flour
½ cup cake flour
⅓ teaspoon baking powder
¼ teaspoon baking soda
1 teaspoon granulated sugar
⅓ teaspoon salt

¼ cup unsalted butter, cubed
½ cup grated cheddar
3 tablespoons scallions, chopped
⅓ cup + 2 tablespoons buttermilk
3 tablespoons butter, melted

1. Sift the baking powder, cake flour, sugar, baking soda, salt, and all-purpose flour in a medium bowl. 2. Make the cubed butter into pea-sized flour with a pastry cutter. 3. Add the scallions and the grated cheddar cheese and toss together to combine well. 4. Stir in the buttermilk to combine the milk and flour to a dough with a rubber spatula. 5. Lightly dust flour over a clean work surface. Press the dough into a ½-inch-thick and 8-inch-wide disk over the prepared surface. 6. Cut out 6 dough rounds from the disk with a 2½-inch round cutter, pressing straight down to avoid twisting. 7. Prepare a baking pan and brush over with a little melted butter. Evenly arrange the biscuits on the pan and brush 1 tablespoon of the melted butter over the biscuits. 8. Cook them in the air fryer at 400°F/200°C for 8 minutes on Air Fry mode, or until the biscuits are golden brown. 9. Serve and enjoy!

Per Serving: Calories 287; Fat 15.1g; Sodium 331mg; Carbs 30.35g; Fiber 1g; Sugar 1.26g; Protein 7.14g

Banana Pecan Bread

⏱ **Prep: 5 minutes**   🍳 **Cook: 40 minutes**   🍃 **Serves: 4**

¼ cup plus 2 teaspoons unsalted butter, room temperature, divided
¾ cup all-purpose flour, plus more for dusting the pan, divided
¼ cup granulated sugar
½ very ripe banana, peeled and mashed
2 large eggs

¾ teaspoon vanilla extract
1 teaspoon ground cinnamon
¼ teaspoon ground nutmeg
¼ teaspoon salt
¼ teaspoon baking soda
⅛ teaspoon baking powder
⅓ cup pecans, chopped and lightly toasted

1. Prepare a loaf pan and grease with 2 teaspoons of butter. Lightly dust the inside of the pan with flour and tap excess flour out. 2. Mix the banana with the remaining butter in a medium mixing bowl with the back of a spoon until mashed and combined well. 3. In a large basin, add the beaten eggs, vanilla essence, nutmeg, cinnamon, salt, and granulated sugar. Stir in ¾ cup of flour, baking powder, and baking soda to form a smooth batter. Fold in pecans and then transfer to the prepared loaf pan. 4. Place the loaf pan in the air fryer, and Bake them at 325°F/165°C for 40 minutes. 5. When cooked, a tester inserted in the banana bread should come out clean. 6. Carefully remove the loaf pan from the air fryer and then invert the loaf. Turn the banana bread right-side up. 7. Slice into your desired size. Serve and enjoy!

Per Serving: Calories 290; Fat 16.32g; Sodium 269mg; Carbs 29.59g; Fiber 2.2g; Sugar 8.52g; Protein 6.97g

Air Fried French Toast

⏱ **Prep: 10 minutes**   🍳 **Cook: 6 minutes**   🍃 **Serves: 2**

4 slices of bread
2 eggs
⅔ cup milk

1 teaspoon vanilla
½ teaspoon cinnamon

1. Beat the eggs in a small bowl, then add in milk, vanilla, and cinnamon, and mix them well. 2. Dip the bread slices with egg mixture, and get off any excess. 3. Prepare a pan and grease with cooking spray, then arrange the bread slices onto the greased pan. 4. Cook them at 320°F/160°C on Air Fry mode for 6 minutes, flipping halfway through. 5. Serve and enjoy!

Per Serving: Calories 511; Fat 27.12g; Sodium 576mg; Carbs 26.21g; Fiber 1.4g; Sugar 7.58g; Protein 36.66g

Easy Scrambled Eggs

⏱ **Prep: 15 minutes**   🍳 **Cook: 5 minutes**   🍃 **Serves: 2**

1 tablespoon butter
2 eggs

1 teaspoon salt
½ teaspoon black pepper

1. Preheat the air fryer at 220°F/105°C on Air Fry mode. 2. Prepare a pan and add the butter to melt in your air fryer for about 1 minute. 3. Mix salt, pepper, and the beaten eggs in a small bowl. 4. Add the egg mixture to the prepared pan and mix with the melted butter, then place the pan in the air fryer. 5. Air fry the mixture for 4 minutes, scraping the pan halfway while cooking. 6. Serve and enjoy!

Per Serving: Calories 116; Fat 9.97g; Sodium 1271mg; Carbs 0.8g; Fiber 0.2g; Sugar 0.17g; Protein 5.66g

Easy Mac & Cheese Casserole

⏲ **Prep: 5 minutes**   🍲 **Cook: 3 hours 10 minutes**   🥬 **Serves: 4**

½ pound Fontina cheese, grated
¼ pound provolone cheese, grated
¼ pound Parmigiano Reggiano cheese, grated
3 tablespoons butter
12 ounces dried ditalini pasta
1½ cups milk

1 (8-ounce) can evaporated milk
1 teaspoon kosher salt
½ teaspoon ground black pepper
2 tablespoons parsley, chopped
½ cup panko breadcrumbs

1. Mix all the cheeses to a large mixing bowl. Reserve half of the cheese mixture. 2. Prepare a suitable casserole dish and grease it. 3. Add pasta, half of the cheese mixture, butter, milk, evaporated milk, black pepper, and salt to the dish. 4. Add parsley on top, and sprinkle with the reserved cheese mixture, then top them with panko breadcrumbs. 5. Firstly cook the food at 275°F/135°C on Slow Cook mode for 3 minutes, then cook them at 400°F/200°C on Broil mode for 10 minutes. 6. When cooked, carefully remove it from the air fryer. 7. Serve and enjoy!

Per Serving: Calories 769; Fat 47.94g; Sodium 2027mg; Carbs 46.63g; Fiber 4.8g; Sugar 9.69g; Protein 38.79g

Cheesy Spinach-Tomato Frittata

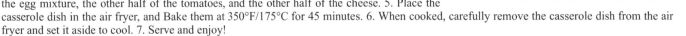

⏲ **Prep: 5 minutes**   🍲 **Cook: 45 minutes**   🥬 **Serves: 8**

24 eggs
½ cup cream
1 tablespoon flour
1 teaspoon salt
½ teaspoon ground black pepper
2 tablespoons butter

1 small onion, sliced thinly
2 cloves garlic, chopped
4 cups baby spinach
6 ounces cherry tomatoes, cut in half
6 ounces feta cheese, crumbled

1. Beat the eggs with add cream, flour, black pepper, and salt in a bowl. Set aside for later use. 2. Melt the butter in the skillet over medium-high heat; add the garlic and onion, and stir them for 2 minutes. 3. Turn off the heat, and add spinach and toss until wilted. 4. Prepare a 4½-quart casserole dish and layer the spinach mixture, half of the tomatoes, half of the feta cheese, the egg mixture, the other half of the tomatoes, and the other half of the cheese. 5. Place the casserole dish in the air fryer, and Bake them at 350°F/175°C for 45 minutes. 6. When cooked, carefully remove the casserole dish from the air fryer and set it aside to cool. 7. Serve and enjoy!

Per Serving: Calories 326; Fat 22.98g; Sodium 714mg; Carbs 8.4g; Fiber 1g; Sugar 5.22g; Protein 20.99g

Garlic Cheese-Broccoli Soufflés

⏲ **Prep: 5 minutes**   🍲 **Cook: 22 minutes**   🥬 **Serves: 6**

5 large eggs
1 clove garlic
¼ cup low-fat cottage cheese
½ teaspoon salt

⅛ teaspoon ground cayenne pepper
2 cups broccoli, finely chopped
¾ cup cheddar cheese, shredded
3 tablespoons scallions, thinly sliced

1. Blend together the beaten eggs, cottage cheese, ground cayenne pepper, garlic, and salt in a blender until a smooth and creamy puree has formed. 2. In a large mixing bowl, pour in the mixture and add cheddar, scallions, and broccoli, and toss them well. 3. Prepare 6 ramekins and brush the inside with butter. 4. Bake them at 300°F/150°C for 22 minutes. 5. When cooked, the soufflés should be puffed and golden brown on top. 6. Carefully remove from the air fryer. Serve and enjoy!

Per Serving: Calories 180; Fat 11.81g; Sodium 639mg; Carbs 4.78g; Fiber 0.5g; Sugar 2.75g; Protein 13.35g

Chive-Cream Cheese Omelet

⏰ **Prep: 5 minutes**   🍱 **Cook: 8 minutes**   🍃 **Serves: 2**

1 tablespoon olive oil
4 large eggs
2 tablespoons minced chives
2 tablespoons water

⅛ teaspoon salt
⅛ teaspoon pepper
2 ounces cream cheese, cubed
Salsa

1. Preheat the air fryer at 350°F/175°C on Roast mode. 2. Beat the eggs with chives, water, pepper, and salt in a medium bowl. 3. Grease a round baking pan with olive oil, then pour in the egg mixture. 4. Let the mixture Roast for 8 minutes, spinning the pan and topping the mixture with the cheese halfway through. 7.When the cooking time is up, carefully remove the omelet from the air fryer. 8.Fold the omelet over and serve with the salsa.

Per Serving: Calories 289; Fat 24.4g; Sodium 440mg; Carbs 2.3g; Fiber 0.2g; Sugar 1.67g; Protein 14.77g

Avocado Egg Boats

⏰ **Prep: 10 minutes**   🍱 **Cook: 10 minutes**   🍃 **Serves: 2**

1 large avocado, halved and pitted
2 large eggs
2 tomato slices, divided

½ cup nonfat Cottage cheese, divided
½ teaspoon fresh cilantro for garnish

1. Slice off a thin bottom piece from each avocado half. 2. To make room for an egg, scoop some flesh from the avocado. 3. Place the avocado halves onto the prepared baking tray, and in each avocado half, break 1 egg. 4. Add one tomato slice and on top ¼ cup of Cottage cheese on top. 5. Bake them in the air fryer at 425°F/220°C for 10 minutes. 6. When cooked, carefully remove it from the air fryer. 7. Serve and enjoy!

Per Serving: Calories 261; Fat 19.62g; Sodium 214mg; Carbs 11.93g; Fiber 6.9g; Sugar 1.91g; Protein 12.17g

Cinnamon Banana Bread Pudding

⏰ **Prep: 10 minutes**   🍱 **Cook: 15 minutes**   🍃 **Serves: 4**

2 medium ripe bananas, mashed
½ cup low-fat milk
2 tablespoons maple syrup
2 tablespoons peanut butter
1 teaspoon vanilla extract

1 teaspoon ground cinnamon
2 slices whole-grain bread, cut into bite-sized cubes
¼ cup quick oats
Cooking spray

1. Lightly spritz a suitable baking dish over with cooking spray. 2. Mix the milk, maple syrup, peanut butter, bananas, vanilla, and cinnamon in a large bowl to incorporate. 3. Stir in the bread cubes and coat the bread cubes completely. 4. Fold in the oats and stir until well combined. Then add into the prepared baking dish. 5. Place the baking dish in the air fryer, and then cook the food at 350°F/175°C on Air Fry mode for 15 minutes. 6. After 10 minutes of cooking time, remove the baking dish, and then return to the air fryer and continue cooking for 5 minutes. 7. When cooked, carefully remove it from the air fryer and let it cool for about 5 minutes. 8. Serve and enjoy!

Per Serving: Calories 231; Fat 6.41g; Sodium mg; Carbs 35.25g; Fiber 4.1g; Sugar 16.4g; Protein 9.3g

Flavorful Vanilla French Toast

⏰ Prep: 10 minutes 🍲 Cook: 5 minutes 🍽 Serves: 4

2 large eggs
2 tablespoons water
⅔ cup whole or 2% milk
1 tablespoon butter, melted

2 tablespoons bourbon
1 teaspoon vanilla extract
8 (1-inch-thick) French bread slices
Cooking spray

1. Line the baking tray with parchment paper, and then spritz with cooking spray. 2. Beat the eggs with water in a shallow bowl, then add the melted butter, bourbon, milk, and vanilla, and mix them well. 3. Dredge 4 slices of bread in the butter mixture and coat well. 4. Then arrange the coated bread onto the paper. 5. Bake the bread slices in the air fryer at 320°F/160°C for 5 minutes until the bread is just nicely browned, flipping them halfway through cooking. 6. Carefully remove the bread slices from the air fryer. 7. Serve and enjoy!

Per Serving: Calories 304; Fat 9.3g; Sodium 388mg; Carbs 36.46g; Fiber 2.3g; Sugar 11.5g; Protein 11.58g

Apple French Toast

⏰ Prep: 15 minutes 🍲 Cook: 55 minutes 🍽 Serves: 8

For the French toast
1-pound challah or raisin challah, sliced into ¾-inch-thick slices
5 large eggs
1½ cups half & half
For the apple topping
4 tablespoons unsalted butter
4 large Granny Smith apples
¼ cup + 2 tablespoons packed dark brown
For serving
Confectioners' sugar and/or maple syrup

3 tablespoons maple syrup
2 tablespoons bourbon
1 teaspoon vanilla extract
¼ teaspoon salt

sugar
6 tablespoons maple syrup
1 teaspoon ground cinnamon

To prepare the toast: 1. Brush the inside of a suitable baking dish with butter. 2. Beat the eggs with half & half, maple syrup, vanilla, salt, and bourbon in a large bowl. 3. Drop the challah slices in the custard mixture for about 5 seconds. Cover the entire bottom of the dish with the overlapped bread slices. 4. Pour in all the remaining ingredients in the dish. Let them sit for later use.
To prepare the apple topping: 1. Peel the apples and cut into thin slices. 2. In a large sauté pan, heat the butter over medium-high heat until melted; add the brown sugar, cinnamon, maple syrup, and apples, and stir them for 8 minutes until the apples are softened and the mixture has thickened. 3. Drizzle all the thickened mixture evenly over the bread. 4. Preheat the air fryer at 350°F/175°C on Bake mode. 5. Cover the dish with aluminum foil, place it in the preheated air fryer, and bake the food for 25 minutes. 6. When the time is up, remove the aluminum foil and resume baking them for 20 minutes until the toasts are puffed and golden. 7. When cooked, carefully remove it from the air fryer. 8. Dust with the confectioners' sugar. Serve and enjoy!

Per Serving: Calories 405; Fat 7.76g; Sodium 135mg; Carbs 82.08g; Fiber 5.2g; Sugar 62.72g; Protein 5.26g

Vanilla Pecan Granola

⏰ Prep: 10 minutes 🍲 Cook: 20 minutes 🍽 Serves: 4

1½ cups rolled oats
¼ cup maple syrup
¼ cup pecan pieces

1 teaspoon vanilla extract
½ teaspoon ground cinnamon

1. Line a baking pan with parchment paper. 2. In a large bowl, mix oats, maple syrup, cinnamon, vanilla, and pecan pieces to coat the oats and the pecan pieces thoroughly. 3. Transfer the mixture onto the prepared baking pan and spread evenly. 4. Bake the mixture at 300°F/150°C for 20 minutes, stirring once halfway through. 5. When cooked, carefully remove it from the air fryer. Allow it to sit to cool for about 30 minutes for serving. 6. Serve and enjoy!

Per Serving: Calories 185; Fat 6.96g; Sodium 4mg; Carbs 37.8g; Fiber 6.2g; Sugar 12.81g; Protein 6.69g

Cheese Spinach & Cherry Tomato Frittata

⏰ **Prep: 10 minutes**   🍲 **Cook: 35 minutes**   🍃 **Serves: 6**

12 eggs
½ cup cheddar cheese, grated
1 ½ cups cherry tomatoes, cut in half
½ cup fresh basil, chopped

1 cup baby spinach, chopped
½ cup yogurt
Salt and pepper to taste

1. Spritz a baking pan with cooking spray. Set it aside for later use. 2. Preheat the air fryer to 390°F/200°C on Bake. 3. Whisk the eggs and yogurt in a large bowl. 4. In the prepared baking pan, layer the spinach, basil, tomatoes, and cheese, and then pour the egg mixture on top. 5. Add salt and pepper to season. 6. Bake the food in the preheated air fryer for 35 minutes. 7. When cooked, carefully remove it from the air fryer. 8. Serve and enjoy!

Per Serving: Calories 177; Fat 10.76g; Sodium 347mg; Carbs 4.88g; Fiber 0.3g; Sugar 3.28g; Protein 14.67g

Chapter 2 Snacks and Appetizers Recipes

Delicious Beef Taquitos

⏰ Prep: 20 minutes   🍲 Cook: 15 minutes   🥢 Serves: 4

2 large eggs
½ cup dry bread crumbs
3 tablespoons taco seasoning

1-pound lean ground beef
4 corn tortillas, warmed
Cooking spray

1. Preheat the air fryer at 350°F/175°C on Air Fry mode. 2. Add bread crumbs, taco seasoning, and eggs to a large mixing bowl and combine well. Then add beef and mix gently until thoroughly coated. 3. Spoon a quarter of the beef mixture in the center of each tortilla. Tightly roll up and use toothpicks to secure. 4. Spritz the cooking tray with cooking spray. 5. Arrange the tortilla evenly on the prepared cooking tray. Spray the cooking spray over the tortillas. 6. Cook them for 15 minutes or until golden brown, flipping them halfway through cooking. 7. When the tortillas are cooked, carefully remove them from the air fryer. 8. Discard the toothpicks to serve.

Per Serving: Calories 490; Fat 18.44g; Sodium 1000mg; Carbs 37.68g; Fiber 2.6g; Sugar 3.2g; Protein 39.15g

Bacon Wrapped Asparagus

⏰ Prep: 10 minutes   🍲 Cook: 15 minutes   🥢 Serves: 6

4 stalks of asparagus (about 10 ounces), trimmed
12 slices of bacon (center-cut preferred)

1 teaspoon olive oil
Garlic salt
Black pepper

1. Trim down the woody ends of the asparagus and evenly drizzle with olive oil. 2. Add garlic, salt, and black pepper to season. 3. Cut the bacon slices lengthwise into narrower strips. 4. Then tightly wrap each bacon trip around an asparagus stalk. 5. Arrange the wrapped asparagus evenly on the cooking tray, then place the tray in the air fryer. 6. Air fry the asparagus at 400°F/200°C for 15 minutes. 7. Carefully remove the tray from the air fryer. Serve and enjoy!

Per Serving: Calories 229; Fat 21.23g; Sodium 246mg; Carbs 2.65g; Fiber 1g; Sugar 1.33g; Protein 7.64g

Dehydrated Gingered Orange Slices

⏰ Prep: 5 minutes   🍲 Cook: 3 hours 5 minutes   🥢 Serves: 15

2 large blood oranges or navel oranges
¼ cup coconut sugar
½ teaspoon ground cinnamon

Pinch of ground ginger
Dash of sea salt

1. Cut the oranges into thin slices. 2. Line the cooking tray with parchment paper. 3. Under running water, wash the oranges. Dry and cut them into slices as thin as possible. Then arrange the slices on the prepared tray. 4. Add sugar and spices to a small mixing bowl and mix well, then sprinkle them over the orange slices. 5. Place the cooking tray in the air fryer. 6. Set the air fryer to Dehydrate function, and adjust the temperature to 200°F/95°C and time to 2-½ to 3 hours, or longer for thick slices. 7. When done, add more spices and sugar as you like. 8. Serve and enjoy!

Per Serving: Calories 19; Fat 0.04g; Sodium 10mg; Carbs 4.7g; Fiber 0.7g; Sugar 3.93g; Protein 0.24g

Cheese Jalapeño Poppers

⏰ **Prep: 10 minutes**   🍲 **Cook: 8 minutes**   🍽 **Serves: 5**

5 fresh medium jalapeños
4 ounces cream cheese, softened
½ cup sharp cheddar cheese, shredded
2 tablespoons green onions, chopped
½ teaspoon garlic powder

¼ teaspoon salt
¼ teaspoon black pepper
¼ cup panko bread crumbs
1 tablespoon butter, melted

1. Cut the jalapenos lengthwise in half. 2. Spoon the seeds and membranes to hollow out the jalapeno halves. Then set aside for later use. 3. Add cream cheese, green onions, salt, garlic powder, black pepper, and sharp cheddar cheese in a small mixing bowl and mix until they are thoroughly combined. 4. Fill the hollow jalapeno halves with the cheese mixture, about 1 tablespoon for each. 5. Add panko bread crumbs and melted butter to a separate small bowl and mix together to evenly coat the bread crumbs with butter. Coat the cream cheese part of the pepper evenly with bread crumbs. 6. Preheat the air fryer at 375°F/190°C on Air Fry mode. 7. Arrange the peppers evenly on the cooking tray, then place the tray in the preheated air fryer. 8. Air fry the peppers for 8 minutes. 9. When the peppers are cooked, carefully remove them from the air fryer. 10. Serve and enjoy!

Per Serving: Calories 205; Fat 16.63g; Sodium 392mg; Carbs 6.83g; Fiber 0.8g; Sugar 3.35g; Protein 8.27g

Crispy Chicken Spring Rolls

⏰ **Prep: 50 minutes**   🍲 **Cook: 35 minutes**   🍽 **Serves: 12**

3 cups coleslaw mix
3 green onions, chopped
1 tablespoon soy sauce
1 teaspoon sesame oil
2 tablespoons Sriracha chili sauce

1-pound boneless skinless chicken breasts
1 teaspoon seasoned salt
2 packages (8-ounce) of softened cream cheese
24 spring roll wrappers
Cooking spray

1. Preheat the air fryer at 360°F/180°C on Air Fry mode. 2. Lightly grease a cooking tray and add the chicken breasts, then place them in the air fryer. 3. While air frying the chicken breasts, mix the green onions, sesame oil, soy sauce, and coleslaw mix in a bowl. 4. When the cooking time is up, carefully remove the chicken from the air fryer. Allow it to cool. 5. On a cutting board, finely chop the chicken and add the seasoned salt. 6. Adjust the cooking temperature to 400°F/200°C and cooking time to 10 to 12 minutes. 7. Add Sriracha chili sauce and cream cheese to a large bowl and mix well. 8. Add coleslaw mixture and chicken pieces to the cheese mixture and stir together until well combined to make the filling. 9. Add 2 tablespoons of the filling mixture to the center of the wrapper and roll from one corner of the wrapper. 10. Roll and seal the edges with water. Repeat with the rest rolls. 11. Arrange the spring rolls evenly onto another greased tray in a single layer and spritz with cooking 12. spray. Cook and flip once halfway through cooking. Spritz the other side with cooking spray. 13. When the spring rolls are cooked, they should be golden brown and crispy. 14. Carefully remove from the air fryer. Serve and enjoy!

Per Serving: Calories 320; Fat 8.07g; Sodium 733mg; Carbs 44.24g; Fiber 1.7g; Sugar 3.21g; Protein 16.48g

Granola Almond Blueberries Mix

⏰ **Prep: 10 minutes**   🍲 **Cook: 30 minutes**   🍽 **Serves: 4**

3½ cups old-fashioned oats
1 cup sliced almonds
½ cup dried blueberries
½ cup golden brown sugar
½ teaspoon salt

¼ teaspoon ground cinnamon
⅓ cup coconut oil
¼ cup honey
2 tablespoons sugar
1½ tablespoon vanilla extract

1. Line the baking pan with parchment paper. 2. Add almonds, brown sugar, cinnamon, salt, blueberries, and oats to a large bowl, toss them well, and then set them aside for later use. 3. In a small saucepan, add oil, sugar, and honey and heat over medium heat to bring to a simmer. Turn off the heat and stir in vanilla. 4. Pour the sugar-honey mixture over the oat mixture and coat evenly, then transfer them together to the baking pan.
5. Bake them at 300°F/150°C for 25 to 30 minutes, stirring every 10 minutes. 6. Carefully remove from the air fryer and press to form a large granola clump with a wooden spatula. 7. Allow the granola to cool until crunchy. 8. Serve and enjoy!

Per Serving: Calories 566; Fat 24.41g; Sodium 296mg; Carbs 105.22g; Fiber 14.3g; Sugar 48.87g; Protein 14.87g

Spiced Pumpkin Strips with Yogurt Sauce

⏰ Prep: 25 minutes   🍲 Cook: 15 minutes   🥘 Serves: 4

½ cup plain Greek yogurt
2 tablespoon maple syrup
2 to 3 teaspoons chipotle peppers in adobo sauce, minced
⅛ teaspoon + ½ teaspoon salt, divided

1 medium pumpkin
¼ teaspoon garlic powder
¼ teaspoon ground cumin
¼ teaspoon chili powder
¼ teaspoon pepper

1. Mix maple syrup, yogurt, chipotle peppers, ⅛ teaspoon of salt, and maple syrup in a small bowl. Cover the bowl and place it in the refrigerator for later use. 2. Lightly grease a tray. 3. Spoon out the seeds. Cut the pumpkins into ½-inch strips and then transfer them to a large bowl. 4. Add ½ teaspoon of salt, cumin, chili powder, pepper, and garlic powder to season the pumpkin strips. 5. Transfer the seasoned strips onto the prepared tray. Place the tray in the air fryer. 6. Cook the food at 400°F/200°C on Air Fry mode for 6 to 8 minutes or until just tender. 7. Carefully remove from the air fryer. 8. Serve with the yogurt sauce and enjoy!

Per Serving: Calories 68; Fat 0.28g; Sodium 110mg; Carbs 13.8g; Fiber 0.6g; Sugar 9.39g; Protein 3.89g

Savory Beef Meatballs

⏰ Prep: 15 minutes   🍲 Cook: 40 minutes   🥘 Serves: 12

Meatballs
1-pound ground beef
1 large egg, beaten lightly
½ cup yellow onion, finely chopped
¼ cup fine dry breadcrumbs
2 tablespoons Parmesan, grated
2 tablespoons milk
2 teaspoons Creole mustard
1 ½ teaspoon garlic, minced
½ teaspoon dried basil
Sauce
1 cup ketchup
½ cup yellow onion, grated
1 teaspoon garlic, minced
¼ cup packed light brown sugar

½ teaspoon dried oregano
½ teaspoon dried parsley
½ teaspoon Creole seasoning
½ teaspoon salt
¼ teaspoon ground black pepper
½ teaspoon Worcestershire sauce
¼ teaspoon hot red pepper sauce
2 teaspoons vegetable oil
2 teaspoons unsalted butter

¼ cup red wine vinegar
1 tablespoon Worcestershire sauce
¼ teaspoon ground black pepper
1 teaspoon salt

1. Add all the meatball ingredients to a suitable mixing bowl and combine well. Form 1-inch balls from the mixture. 2. Arrange the meatballs on a baking tray, and then place the tray in the air fryer. 3. Cook the meatballs at 400°F/200°C on Air Fry mode for 10 minutes. 4. Mix together ketchup, yellow onion, minced garlic, brown sugar, red wine vinegar, Worcestershire sauce, black pepper, and salt in a mixing bowl. Whisk until the sugar has dissolved. 5. When cooked, transfer the meatballs to a casserole dish and drizzle with the sauce mixture. Cover the dish, and place them back in the air fryer. 6. Bake them at 325°F/165°C for 30 minutes. 7. When baked, serve and enjoy!

Per Serving: Calories 158; Fat 6.41g; Sodium 552mg; Carbs 13.69g; Fiber 0.6g; Sugar 10.38g; Protein 11.59g

Crispy Avocado Slices

⏰ Prep: 10 minutes   🍲 Cook: 10 minutes   🥘 Serves: 4

1 large avocado, pitted, peeled, and cut into ½-inch slices
1 egg
1-⅓ tablespoons lime juice
¼ teaspoon hot sauce

3 tablespoons flour
¾ cup panko bread crumbs
¼ cup cornmeal
¼ teaspoon salt
Cooking spray

1. In a small bowl, add lime juice, hot sauce, and egg and mix well. 2. In a bowl, add flour. In a second bowl, add the salt, cornmeal, and bread crumbs and combine well. 3. Dip the avocado slice first in the flour, then in the egg mixture, and finally coat with bread crumb mixture. 4. Arrange the coated avocado slices onto the cooking tray and spritz with cooking spray. 5. Set the air fryer to the Air Fry function, and adjust the temperature to 390°F/200°C and time to 10 minutes. 6. Press Start/Stop to begin. 7. Cook them at 390°F/200°C on Air Fry mode for 10 minutes until crispy and golden brown. 8. When done, serve and enjoy!

Per Serving: Calories 235; Fat 9.72g; Sodium 322mg; Carbs 31.45g; Fiber 4.8g; Sugar 1.85g; Protein 6.41g

Cheese Bacon Stuffed Jalapeño Peppers

🕐 Prep: 10 minutes   🍲 Cook: 15 minutes   🥞 Serves: 8

16 jalapeños peppers
4 ounces cream cheese, room temperature
½ cup Monterey Jack cheese, grated
6 strips bacon, cooked and crumbled
2 teaspoons Creole seasoning

½ cup milk
1 egg, beaten lightly
½ cup plus 3 tablespoons all-purpose flour
1½ cups panko breadcrumbs
Sea salt, for serving

1. Cut slits lengthwise down one side of the jalapenos and reserve the stem. Spoon some seeds out from the jalapeno. 2. In a small bowl, add cheese, cream cheese, ½ teaspoon of the Creole seasoning, and bacon, and mix until well combined. 3. In a resealable plastic food storage bag, fill halfway with the cheese mixture. 4. Squeeze the cheese mixture to the bottom of the bag and fill each pepper. Fold the slits together. 5. Add egg, milk, and ½ cup of flour to a mixing bowl. In a separate bowl, add the remaining flour and the remaining Creole spice and panko breadcrumbs and combine well. 6. Drop the stuffed jalapenos in the milk batter and evenly coat with panko mixture. Press to coat well. 7. Arrange the jalapenos evenly on the cooking tray, then place the tray in the air fryer. 8. Air Fry them at 400°F/200°C for 15 minutes. 9. When cooked, add salt to season. Serve and enjoy!

Per Serving: Calories 248; Fat 10.01g; Sodium 387mg; Carbs 31.02g; Fiber 2.7g; Sugar 7.27g; Protein 9.94g

Crunchy Onion Rings

🕐 Prep: 10 minutes   🍲 Cook: 18 minutes   🥞 Serves: 2

1½ teaspoons kosher salt
½ teaspoon freshly ground black pepper
1 cup all-purpose flour
1 teaspoon paprika
½ teaspoon onion powder
½ teaspoon garlic powder

⅛ teaspoon cayenne
1½ cups panko breadcrumbs
2 large eggs, beaten
1 medium yellow onion, sliced into ½-inch rings
Marinara sauce, for serving

1. Whisk salt, flour, pepper, onion powder, cayenne, garlic powder, and paprika in a medium bowl. 2. Add the panko bread crumbs to a shallow dish. In a separate bowl, add the eggs. 3. Dip the onion rings first in the flour, then in the eggs, and finally in the bread crumbs. Press to coat them well. 4. Arrange the onion rings on the cooking tray, then cook them at 400°F/200°C on Air Fry mode for 18 minutes. 5. You can air fry the onion rings in batches. 6. When done, carefully remove the tray from the air fryer. 7. Serve and enjoy!

Per Serving: Calories 630; Fat 9.87g; Sodium 2411mg; Carbs 108.85g; Fiber 6.2g; Sugar 5.7g; Protein 24.03g

Cheddar Jalapeño Cornbread

🕐 Prep: 10 minutes   🍲 Cook: 30 minutes   🥞 Serves: 8

1½ cups all-purpose flour
1½ cups yellow cornmeal
1½ tablespoons baking powder
1½ teaspoons salt
¼ teaspoon ground cayenne pepper
1½ cups whole milk
3 large eggs
½ cup sharp cheddar, grated

1½ tablespoons green jalapeño, seeds and stems removed, minced
1½ tablespoons red jalapeño, seeds and stems removed, minced
⅓ cup plus 1 tablespoon vegetable oil, divided
1½ tablespoons honey
½ tablespoon butter

1. Whisk cornmeal, baking powder, ground cayenne pepper, salt, and flour in a large mixing bowl. 2. Add milk, cheddar, ¼ cup of vegetable oil, jalapeno, and eggs to a separate bowl, and then stir them until well combined. 3. Prepare an oven-safe baking dish and add 1 tablespoon of vegetable oil. Then add the batter to fill halfway. 4. Place the baking dish in the air fryer, and Bake the food at 325°F/165°C for 30 minutes or until a toothpick inserted comes out clean from the bread and lightly golden brown on its top.5. Carefully remove the dish from the air fryer and brush the honey and butter over the top. 6. Allow it to cool before serving. 7. Serve and enjoy!

Per Serving: Calories 407; Fat 15.67g; Sodium 611mg; Carbs 55.88g; Fiber 2.8g; Sugar 9.98g; Protein 11.41g

Crunchy Spicy Chickpeas

⏰ Prep: 10 minutes 🍲 Cook: 18 minutes 🥢 Serves: 4

1 (19-ounces) can of chickpeas, drained and rinsed
½ teaspoon chili powder
½ teaspoon ground cumin

¼ teaspoon cayenne pepper
¼ teaspoon salt
Cooking spray

1. Line the cooking tray with parchment paper and lightly spritz with cooking spray. 2. Mix chili powder, cayenne pepper, salt, and cumin in a small bowl. 3. Add chickpeas to a medium bowl, and spritz with cooking spray. 4. Mix together the spice mixture with the chickpeas and toss to coat well. 5. Transfer the spiced chickpeas to the prepared cooking tray. 6. Air Fry the chickpeas at 390°F/200°C for 18 minutes, stirring them twice halfway through cooking. 7. When the chickpeas are cooked, the chickpeas should be crunchy. 8. Carefully remove the tray from the air fryer. 9. Cool the chickpeas for about 5 minutes. 10. Serve and enjoy!

Per Serving: Calories 90; Fat 1.88g; Sodium 311mg; Carbs 14.62g; Fiber 4.2g; Sugar 2.58g; Protein 4.57g

Mini Cheese Sausage Pizzas

⏰ Prep: 5 minutes 🍲 Cook: 30 minutes 🥢 Serves: 4

1-pound semolina pizza dough
3½ cups tomato sauce
1½ pounds hot Italian sausage, casings removed and meat crumbled
8 ounces mozzarella, grated

2 tablespoons fresh thyme leaves, chopped
½ teaspoon crushed red pepper
¼ cup Parmigiano-Reggiano, finely grated
Extra-virgin olive oil for drizzling (optional)

1. Divide the dough into 4 equal parts. 2. Lightly dust flour over a work surface. Knead the 4 equal parts into an 8-inch round. 3. Add the sausage to the cooking tray, then place the tray in the air fryer. 4. Air Fry the sausages at 400°F/200°C for 15 minutes. 5.When the sausages are completely cooked, carefully remove them from the tray, and set aside for later use. 6. Place one dough portion at a time on the tray. Spread one-quarter of the tomato sauce, mozzarella, and the cooked sausage on each dough portion. 7. Add thyme, crushed red pepper, and Parmigiano-Reggiano to garnish. 8. Working in batches, bake the dough at 400°F/200°C for 15 minutes or until crispy. 9.Drizzle with some extra olive oil to serve as you like.

Per Serving: Calories 887; Fat 55.17g; Sodium 2088mg; Carbs 47.62g; Fiber 6.9g; Sugar 12.99g; Protein 51.26g

Roasted Cheese Potato Skins

⏰ Prep: 10 minutes 🍲 Cook: 20 minutes 🥢 Serves: 6

12 small red potatoes
1 teaspoon Kosher salt, divided
1 tablespoon extra-virgin olive oil
¼ cup grated sharp Cheddar cheese

¼ cup sour cream
2 tablespoons chopped chives
2 tablespoons grated Parmesan cheese

1. Place the potatoes in a large bowl, then toss them with ½ teaspoon of salt and olive. 2. Evenly arrange the potatoes in the baking pan, then place the pan in the air fryer. 3. Roast the potatoes at 375°F/190°C for 15 minutes; after 10 minutes of cooking time, flip them. 4. When done, remove the pan and let the potatoes rest for 5 minutes. 5. Halve the potatoes lengthwise. 6. Using a spoon, scoop the potato into a bowl, leaving a thin shell of skin. Arrange the potato halves on the baking pan. 7. Mash the potato flesh until smooth. Stir in the remaining ½ teaspoon of the salt, Cheddar cheese, sour cream, and chives. 8. Spoon the filling into the potato shells; sprinkle them with Parmesan cheese. 9. Roast them at 375°F/190°C for 5 minutes. 10. When cooking is complete, the tops should be browning slightly. 11. Remove the potatoes and let them cool slightly before serving.

Per Serving: Calories 623; Fat 9.91g; Sodium 700mg; Carbs 118.7g; Fiber 12.6g; Sugar 9.61g; Protein 19.38g

Simple Fried Plantain Pieces

⏰ **Prep: 10 minutes** 🍲 **Cook: 10 minutes** 🥬 **Serves: 2**

2 ripe plantains, peeled and cut at a diagonal into ½ inch thick pieces

3 tablespoons ghee, melted
¼ teaspoon kosher salt

1. Add salt, ghee, and plantains to a bowl. 2. Then add the seasoned plantains to the cooking tray. 3. Cook the plantains at 400°F/200°C on Air Fry mode for 8 minutes. 4. When done, the plantains should be soft on the inside and crispy on the outside. 5. Carefully remove them from the air fryer. 6. Serve and enjoy!

Per Serving: Calories 371; Fat 17.94g; Sodium 300mg; Carbs 57.1g; Fiber 4.1g; Sugar 26.86g; Protein 2.51g

Chapter 3 Vegetables and Sides Recipes

Lemony Brussels Sprouts with Sun-Dried Tomatoes

⏱ Prep: 10 minutes   🍲 Cook: 20 minutes   🍃 Serves: 4

1 pound Brussels sprouts, trimmed and halved
1 tablespoon extra-virgin olive oil
Sea salt and freshly ground black pepper to taste
½ cup sun-dried tomatoes, chopped
2 tablespoons freshly squeezed lemon juice
1 teaspoon lemon zest

1. Add the Brussels sprouts to a large bowl, and then evenly coat them with olive oil, salt, and pepper. 2. Transfer the Brussels sprouts to the baking pan in a single layer. 3. Roast them in the air fryer at 400°F/200°C for 20 minutes until they are caramelized. 4. Transfer the Brussels sprouts to a bowl and toss with the tomatoes, lemon juice, and lemon zest. 5. Serve immediately.

Per Serving: Calories 83; Fat 2.08g; Sodium 75mg; Carbs 14.89g; Fiber 5.3g; Sugar 5.26g; Protein 4.89g

Breaded Garlicky Brussels Sprouts

⏱ Prep: 10 minutes   🍲 Cook: 20 minutes   🍃 Serves: 2

1 tablespoon olive oil
2 garlic cloves, minced
½ teaspoon salt
¼ teaspoon black pepper
1 pound Brussels sprouts, trimmed and halved
½ cup panko breadcrumbs
1-½ teaspoons fresh rosemary, minced

1. Preheat your air fryer at 350°F/175°C. 2. Mix up the oil, garlic, salt, and pepper in a bowl, and then heat for 30 seconds in the microwave. 3. In another bowl, add the Brussels sprouts and two tablespoons of the garlic mixture, and mix them well. 4. Spread the sprouts in the cooking tray. 5. Air Fry the Brussels sprouts at 220°F/105°C for 18 minutes; after 5 minutes of cooking, toss the sprouts well, and then resume air frying them for 8 minutes. 6. Mix the remaining oil mixture with rosemary and breadcrumbs. 7. Spread this mixture over the Brussels sprouts and then resume air frying for 5 minutes. 8. Enjoy.

Per Serving: Calories 270; Fat 8.9g; Sodium 836mg; Carbs 41g; Fiber 10g; Sugar 6.7g; Protein 11.51g

Roasted Brussels Sprouts with Parmesan Cheese

⏱ Prep: 10 minutes   🍲 Cook: 30 minutes   🍃 Serves: 4

1 pound Brussels sprouts, rinsed and dried, ends trimmed, sliced in half lengthwise
2 tablespoons extra virgin olive oil
2–3 cloves garlic, minced
2 teaspoons fresh lemon juice, plus more for serving
½ teaspoon fine sea salt
¼ teaspoon freshly ground black pepper
¼ cup parmesan cheese, freshly grated

1. Select the Air Fry setting to 400°F/200°C and preheat the air fryer. 2. Tossing the Brussels sprouts with the garlic, lemon juice, olive oil, salt and pepper in the large mixing bowl. 3. Spread the Brussels sprouts onto the baking pan in an even layer. 4. Air Fry the Brussels sprouts at 400°F/200°C for 30 minutes, tossing them halfway through cooking. 5. When done, sprinkle with grated parmesan cheese. Serve and enjoy.

Per Serving: Calories 105; Fat 5.1g; Sodium 492mg; Carbs 11.8g; Fiber 4.4g; Sugar 2.58g; Protein 5.76g

Cheese Bacon Loaded Potato Boats

⏰ **Prep: 30 minutes** 🍲 **Cook: 1 hour 20 minutes** 🍃 **Serves: 12**

8 baking potatoes, washed
3 tablespoons canola oil
2 sticks of salted butter
1 cup sour cream
1 cup bacon bits
1 cup cheddar or Jack cheese plus more for

topping
1 cup whole Milk
2 teaspoons seasoned salt
3 green onions, sliced
Freshly ground black pepper

1. Place the potatoes on the baking sheet, coat them with the canola oil, and then bake them in the air fryer at 400°F/200°C for an hour or until cooked through. 2. Slice the butter into pats, and then mix with the bacon bits and sour cream in a large mixing bowl. 3. When the potatoes are done, cut them in half lengthwise and then scrape out the insides into the butter mixture. Mix them well with the cheese, milk, onions, salt, and black pepper. 4. Leave a small rim of potato intact for support. 5. Lay the hollowed-out potato shells on the baking pan, fill these potato shells with the filling and top them with a little more grated cheese. 6. Place the pan in the air fryer. 7. Bake them in the air fryer at 350°F/175°C for 20 minutes. 8. When done, serve and enjoy.

Per Serving: Calories 362; Fat 12.58g; Sodium 668mg; Carbs 51.46g; Fiber 6.7g; Sugar 5.37g; Protein 12.16g

Air Fried Corn with Cheese

⏰ **Prep: 5 minutes** 🍲 **Cook: 10 minutes** 🍃 **Serves: 4**

½ cup sour cream
2 tablespoons whole Milk
4 ears of fresh sweet corn, silk, and husks removed
3 tablespoons butter, melted

1 lime, halved
½ cup Parmesan cheese, finely grated
1 tablespoon chili powder
1½ teaspoons kosher salt

1. Mix up the sour cream and milk in the bowl, then set aside for later use. 2. Cut the corn in half and generously brush them with the melted butter; arrange them on the cooking tray, and then place the tray in the air fryer. 3. Cook the corns at 400°F/200°C on Air Fry mode for 8 minutes until they are crisp-tender and lightly golden in places. 4. Transfer the corn to a platter and squeeze the lime over the cooked corn. 5. Brush the corns with some of the sour cream mixtures. Coat the corn evenly on all sides with the cheese, sprinkle the corn with the chili powder and kosher salt; enjoy.

Per Serving: Calories 304; Fat 17.39g; Sodium 1272mg; Carbs 33.27g; Fiber 4.6g; Sugar 5.39g; Protein 9.81g

Yogurt-Flavored Sweet Potato Wedges

⏰ **Prep: 5 minutes** 🍲 **Cook: 20 minutes** 🍃 **Serves: 8**

5 sweet potatoes, washed and cut into wedges
½ cup plain yogurt
Spice mixture:
1 teaspoon garlic powder

2 tablespoons dried buttermilk
Olive oil spray

Salt and pepper to taste

1. Microwave the sweet potatoes on high heat for 2 minutes, and then let them cool. 2. Cut the cooled sweet potatoes into wedges, brush them with the yogurt, then place them in the cooking tray in a single layer. 3. Mix up the garlic powder, salt, and pepper in a bowl. 4. Dust the sweet potatoes with the dried buttermilk and garlic powder mixture, then spray them with some olive oil spray. 5. Place the cooking tray in the air fryer. 6. Air Fry the food at 400°F/200°C for 18 minutes, flipping them halfway through. 7. When done, serve and enjoy.

Per Serving: Calories 84; Fat 0.59g; Sodium 60mg; Carbs 18.06g; Fiber 2.6g; Sugar 4.59g; Protein 2.11g

Easy Dehydrated Plum Tomatoes

⏰ Prep: 5 minutes   🍲 Cook: 10 hours   🥬 Serves: 6

15 plum tomatoes, halved

1. Place the sliced tomatoes on the cooking tray, then place the tray in the air fryer. 2. Dehydrate the tomatoes at 145°F/60°C for 10 hours. 3. When done, the tomato halves should be crisp.

Per Serving: Calories 102; Fat 0.12g; Sodium mg; Carbs 26.73g; Fiber 1g; Sugar 25.66g; Protein 0.41g

Air Fried Paprika Cauliflower

⏰ Prep: 10 minutes   🍲 Cook: 20 minutes   🥬 Serves: 4

1 large head cauliflower, cut into pieces or broken into small florets
2 teaspoons smoked paprika

1 teaspoon garlic powder
Salt and black pepper to taste
Cooking spray

1. Spray the cooking tray with cooking spray. 2. Evenly coat the cauliflower florets with smoked paprika, garlic powder, salt, and pepper. 3. Place the cauliflower florets in the tray, and then lightly mist them with cooking spray. 4. Air Fry the cauliflower florets at 400°F/200°C for 20 minutes. 5. Stir the cauliflower four times during cooking. 6. When done, serve hot.

Per Serving: Calories 27; Fat 0.36g; Sodium 22mg; Carbs 5.54g; Fiber 2g; Sugar 1.98g; Protein 1.79g

Breaded Parmesan Green Beans

⏰ Prep: 10 minutes   🍲 Cook: 15 minutes   🥬 Serves: 4

½ cup wheat flour
2 eggs
1 cup panko bread crumbs
½ cup grated Parmesan cheese

1 teaspoon cayenne pepper
Salt and black pepper to taste
1½ pounds of green beans

1. Add the flour to a bowl. 2. Lightly beat the eggs into another bowl. 3. Thoroughly mix the bread crumbs, cheese, salt, cayenne pepper, and black pepper in the third bowl. 4. Dip the green beans in the flour, then in the beaten eggs, and finally in the bread crumb mixture to coat well. 5. Transfer the green beans to the cooking tray. 6. Air Fry the green beans at 400°F/200°C for 15 minutes, stirring them halfway through. 7. When cooked, serve.

Per Serving: Calories 306; Fat 7.63g; Sodium 466mg; Carbs 46.43g; Fiber 6.5g; Sugar 7.97g; Protein14.93g

Italian Seasoned Zucchini Sticks

⏰ Prep: 10 minutes   🍲 Cook: 20 minutes   📚 Serves: 6

2 pounds zucchini
3 tablespoons olive oil
½ teaspoon Italian seasoning

½ teaspoon garlic powder
½ teaspoon sea salt
¼ teaspoon black pepper

1. Cutaway the ends of zucchini and then cut each one across in half; cut each piece four times lengthwise. 2. Mix the zucchini sticks with olive oil, then season with Italian seasoning, salt, pepper, and garlic powder. 3. Arrange the zucchini sticks in a single layer on the baking pan. 4. Roast the zucchini sticks at 400°F/200°C for 20 minutes, flipping them halfway through cooking. 5. Serve directly.

Per Serving: Calories 93; Fat 7.36g; Sodium 215mg; Carbs 5.11g; Fiber 1.7g; Sugar 0.03g; Protein 4.16g

Crispy Kale Chips

⏰ Prep: 5 minutes   🍲 Cook: 25 minutes   📚 Serves: 4

1 large bundle of curly green or purple kale   oil
1 to 2 tablespoons Melted coconut or avocado   Seasonings of choice

1. Preheat the air fryer at 225°F/105°C on Bake mode. 2. Rinse and dry the kale thoroughly, tear it into small pieces and discard the stems. 3. Thoroughly combine the kale pieces with the oil and the seasoning of your choice in a mixing bowl. 4. Arrange the kale pieces on the baking pan. Ensure that the kale touches as little as possible. 5. Bake the kale pieces for 25 minutes. 6. After 15 minutes of cooking time, turn the kale pieces over and bake for another 5 to 10 minutes. 7. Let the kale chips cool for a while before serving.

Per Serving: Calories 65; Fat 4.02g; Sodium 78mg; Carbs 6.28g; Fiber 2.5g; Sugar 1.59g; Protein 2.9g

Cheese Broccoli Stuffed Mushrooms

⏰ Prep: 20 minutes   🍲 Cook: 20 minutes   📚 Serves: 4-6

¼ cup grated processed cheese
½ cup grated broccoli
2 teaspoons butter
14 large-sized button mushrooms

1 teaspoon finely chopped garlic
1 teaspoon finely chopped green chilies
¼ cup finely chopped onions
Salt to taste

1. Remove the stems from the mushrooms, discard the stems and wash the mushroom caps. 2. Heat the butter in the nonstick pan over medium heat; add green chilies, garlic and onions and sauté for 2 minutes; add the broccoli and salt and sauté for 4 minutes. 3. Turn off the heat, add cheese, mix well, and divide this mixture into 14 portions. 4. Stuff the mushroom caps with the portions. 5. Bake the food in the air fryer at 400°F/200°C for 10 minutes. 6. When done, serve warm.

Per Serving: Calories 44; Fat 2.73g; Sodium 72mg; Carbs 2.51g; Fiber 0.7g; Sugar 1.31g; Protein 3.25g

Air-Fried Lemon Garlic Broccoli

⏰ Prep: 5 minutes   🍲 Cook: 20 minutes   🥬 Serves: 4

12 ounces broccoli
1 tablespoon olive oil
1 tablespoon lemon juice

1 clove garlic minced
½ teaspoon Kosher salt

1. Rinse and shake dry the broccoli, then trim the tips. 2. Toss the broccoli with lemon juice, salt, olive oil, and garlic in a mixing bowl. 3. Arrange the broccoli in a single layer on the baking pan. 4. Roast the broccoli at 380°F/195°C for 7 minutes. 5. When done, serve immediately.

Per Serving: Calories 51; Fat 3.8g; Sodium 319mg; Carbs 2.94g; Fiber 2.3g; Sugar 0.43g; Protein 2.76g

Honey-Roasted Parsnips with Cheese Dip

⏰ Prep: 25 minutes   🍲 Cook: 1 hour   🥬 Serves: 6-8

3 or 4 parsnips, cut into long fingers
4 tablespoons olive oil
For the dip:
1 cup Mascarpone
1 cup Greek yogurt
2 ounces Asiago Cheese

4 tablespoons clear honey

2 tablespoons extra-virgin olive oil
2 crushed garlic cloves
A few fresh thyme sprigs

To make the parsnips: 1. Coat the parsnips with the olive oil in the baking pan and spread out. 2. Roast the coated parsnips in the air fryer at 390°F/200°C for 20 minutes. 3. When the time is up, take the pan out, drizzle the parsnips with the honey, and then roast them for 15 minutes.
To make the dip: 1. In an ovenproof dish, Mix all the dip ingredients in an ovenproof dish to make the dip. 2. Cook the dip in the oven for 25 minutes; after 15 minutes of cooking time, check the dip and then continue cooking. 3. Serve the parsnips with the dip.

Per Serving: Calories 282; Fat 16.05g; Sodium mg; Carbs 29.03g; Fiber 4.9g; Sugar 15.45g; Protein 7.56g

Cheese Spinach-Zucchini Casserole

⏰ Prep: 10 minutes   🍲 Cook: 40 minutes   🥬 Serves: 6

3 cups baby spinach
2 teaspoons garlic powder
2 egg whites
1 teaspoon dried basil
1 tablespoon olive oil
½ cup breadcrumbs

2 small zucchinis, diced
¼ cup Parmesan cheese, grated
2 small yellow squash, diced
¼ cup feta cheese, crumbled
Salt and pepper

1. In the skillet over medium heat, Heat the olive oil in the skillet over medium heat; add the yellow squash and zucchini, and sauté them for 5 minutes. Add the spinach and cook until the spinach is wilted. 2. Drain any excess liquid and then transfer the sautéed zucchini mixture to the mixing bowl. 3. Add the remaining ingredients to the mixing bowl and mix them with the zucchini mixture until well combined. 4. Transfer the mixture to the baking pan. 5. Bake the food at 400°F/200°C for 40 minutes. 6. When cooked, transfer the food to the serving plate.

Per Serving: Calories 110; Fat 5.4g; Sodium 230mg; Carbs 10.42g; Fiber 1.4g; Sugar 1.85g; Protein 5.71g

Herbed Zucchini Slices & Bell Peppers

🕙 **Prep: 10 minutes**　🍲 **Cook: 25 minutes**　🍃 **Serves: 4**

2 pounds zucchini, sliced
2 tablespoons dried herbs
2 garlic cloves, sliced
1 tablespoon canola oil

1-pound bell peppers, sliced
Pepper
Salt

1. Coat the zucchini and bell peppers with the oil, garlic, dried herbs, salt, and pepper in a large bowl. 2. Spread the coated zucchini and bell peppers onto the baking pan. 3. Bake them at 400°F/200°C for 25 minutes, stirring them halfway through cooking. 4. When done, serve and enjoy.

Per Serving: Calories 126; Fat 4.64g; Sodium 54mg; Carbs 18.31g; Fiber 4.2g; Sugar 5.8g; Protein 8.51g

Cheese-Herb Stuffed Tomato Halves

🕙 **Prep: 10 minutes**　🍲 **Cook: 15 minutes**　🍃 **Serves: 4**

4 large tomatoes, halved
¼ cup fresh oregano, chopped
¼ cup fresh basil, chopped
½ cup mozzarella cheese, shredded

¼ cup Parmesan cheese, grated
Pepper
Salt

1. Arrange the tomato halves to the baking pan, cut-side up. 2. Top the tomato halves with Parmesan cheese, mozzarella cheese, basil, oregano, salt, and pepper. 3. Bake them at 450°F/230°C for 15 minutes. 4. When done, transfer the food to the serving plate.

Per Serving: Calories 84; Fat 2.19g; Sodium 266mg; Carbs 9.74g; Fiber 3.2g; Sugar 5.08g; Protein 8.07g

Herb-Garlic Carrots & Turnips

🕙 **Prep: 10 minutes**　🍲 **Cook: 25 minutes**　🍃 **Serves: 4**

1-pound turnips, peeled and cut into 1–2-inch pieces
1-pound carrots, peeled and cut into 1–2-inch pieces
2 tablespoons canola oil

1 tablespoon dried herbs
2 garlic cloves, sliced
Pepper
Salt

1. Add the turnip and carrot pieces to a large and deep bowl, then toss them with the oil, dried herbs, garlic, salt, and pepper. 2. Spread them onto the baking pan. 3. Bake them at 450°F/230°C for 25 minutes, stirring them halfway through. 4. When done, transfer the food to the serving plate.

Per Serving: Calories 150; Fat 7.71g; Sodium 139mg; Carbs 16.88g; Fiber 6.7g; Sugar 6.6g; Protein 4.54g

Cheese Broccoli Casserole

🕐 Prep: 10 minutes 🍲 Cook: 10 minutes 🍃 Serves: 6

20 ounces fresh broccoli florets, steamed
¼ cup Monterey jack cheese, shredded
1 tablespoon ranch seasoning
¼ cup sour cream

1 cup cheddar cheese, shredded
8 ounces cream cheese, softened
Pepper
Salt

1. Combine the broccoli, ranch seasoning, sour cream, cheddar cheese, cream cheese, salt, and pepper in a bowl. 2. Transfer the mixture to the baking pan and then top with the shredded Monterey jack cheese. 3. Bake the mixture at 350°F/175°C for 10 minutes. 4. When done, transfer the food to the serving plate.

Per Serving: Calories 237; Fat 17.31g; Sodium 783mg; Carbs 9.62g; Fiber 2.7g; Sugar 4.55g; Protein 12.5g

Buttered Acorn Squash Slices

🕐 Prep: 10 minutes 🍲 Cook: 15 minutes 🍃 Serves: 4

1 acorn squash, seeds removed and cut into slices
1 stick butter, melted

¼ cup maple syrup
¼ teaspoon kosher salt

1. Toss the acorn squash slices with maple syrup, salt, and butter, then arrange the acorn squash slices in the baking pan. 2. Air Fry the slices at 400°F/200°C for 15 minutes, turning them halfway through cooking. 3.When the time is up, allow the food to cool slightly before serving.

Per Serving: Calories 297; Fat 23.03g; Sodium 333mg; Carbs 24.45g; Fiber 1.6g; Sugar 11.93g; Protein 1.11g

Chapter 4 Fish and Seafood Recipes

Lemon-Garlic Shrimp

🕐 **Prep: 10 minutes**   🍲 **Cook: 10 minutes**   🍃 **Serves: 4**

8 ounces of medium shelled and deveined shrimp
1 medium lemon

2 tablespoons unsalted butter, melted
½ teaspoon minced garlic
½ teaspoon Old bay seasoning

1. Peel the lemon and then cut in half. 2. Place shrimp in a large bowl and squeeze juice from ½ lemon on top of them. 3. Mix the lemon zest with the remaining ingredients in a bowl. 4. Coat the shrimp with the lemon zest mixture until fully coated. 5. Pour bowl contents into the baking pan, then place the pan in the air fryer. 6. Air Fry the shrimp at 400°F/205°C for 6 minutes until they are bright pink. 7. Serve warm.

Per Serving: Calories 79; Fat 4.47g; Sodium 324mg; Carbs 1.52g; Fiber 0.1g; Sugar 0.31g; Protein 8.02g

Breaded Fish Fillets

🕐 **Prep: 5 minutes**   🍲 **Cook: 20 minutes**   🍃 **Serves: 8**

8 (28 ounces) fish fillets
1 tablespoon olive oil
1 cup dry breadcrumbs
½ teaspoon paprika
¼ teaspoon chili powder

¼ teaspoon ground black pepper
¼ teaspoon garlic powder or granules
¼ teaspoon onion powder
½ teaspoon salt

1. Arrange the fish fillets on the work surface, and coat them with olive oil. 2. Mix paprika, garlic powder, bread crumbs, chili powder, salt, and onion powder in a mixing bowl. 3. Coat each fillet with the breadcrumbs mixture and transfer them to the cooking tray. 4. Air Fry the fillets at 390°F/200°C for 16 minutes. 5. After 8 to 10 minutes of cooking time, turn over the fillets and resume cooking for 5 to 6 minutes. 6. When done, serve warm.

Per Serving: Calories 205; Fat 11.15g; Sodium 222mg; Carbs 7.39g; Fiber 1.1g; Sugar 6.18g; Protein 18.5g

Yummy Tuna Patties

🕐 **Prep: 10 minutes**   🍲 **Cook: 15 minutes**   🍃 **Serves: 2**

1 teaspoon garlic powder
2 cans tuna in water
1 teaspoon dill seasoning
4 teaspoons all-purpose flour
¼ teaspoon salt

4 teaspoons mayonnaise
2 tablespoons lemon juice
½ teaspoon onion powder
¼ teaspoon pepper

1. Add the almond flour, onion powder, garlic powder, mayonnaise, dill, salt, and pepper to the blender, then blend them for about 30 seconds until incorporated. 2. Add the tuna and lemon juice to the blender and then pulse for 30 seconds again until incorporated. 3. Form 4 patties from the mixture and transfer them to the baking pan. 4. Bake the patties at 400°F/200°C for 12 minutes. 5. When done, serve immediately.

Per Serving: Calories 208; Fat 5.03g; Sodium 777mg; Carbs 7.7g; Fiber 0.8g; Sugar 0.56g; Protein 33.78g

Baked Lemon Garlic Sardines

⏰ Prep: 15 minutes 🍲 Cook: 45 minutes 🍴 Serves: 6

2½ pounds sardines
Salt and ground black pepper to taste
2 tablespoons Rigani (Greek oregano)
5 to 6 garlic cloves

½ cup olive oil
½ cup squeezed lemon juice
½ cup water

1. Remove the scales and intestines of the sardines, and leave the heads intact. 2. Arrange the sardines in the baking pan and then evenly sprinkle them with the remaining ingredients. 3. Bake the sardines at 355°F/180°C for 45 minutes. 4. When done, serve and enjoy.

Per Serving: Calories 568; Fat 39.79g; Sodium 583mg; Carbs 4.18g; Fiber 1g; Sugar 0.99g; Protein 47.07g

Tasty Salmon Fillets

⏰ Prep: 25 minutes 🍲 Cook: 20 minutes 🍴 Serves: 4

4 (6 ounces) Salmon fillets
½ cup Soy sauce
¼ cup Brown sugar
1 teaspoon Garlic powder

½ teaspoon Ground ginger
1 tablespoon Cornstarch
1 tablespoon sesame seeds
2 finely chopped scallions

1. Mix the brown sugar, garlic powder, soy sauce, ginger, and cornstarch in a large bowl. 2. Place the fillets in the bowl and coat them with the mixture totally; let the fillets marinate for 20 minutes. 3. Line the baking pan with parchment paper and place the marinated fillets to the pan. 4. Bake the fillets at 350°F/175°C for 20 minutes. 5. While baking the fillets, in the saucepan over medium heat, heat the leftover marinade until it thickens. 6. When the fillets are done, take them out and spread the marinade over them. 7. Top this dish with the sesame seeds and scallions, and enjoy.

Per Serving: Calories 222; Fat 8.63g; Sodium 510mg; Carbs 24.75g; Fiber1.2 g; Sugar 19.7g; Protein 11.55g

Delectable Feta Seafood Stew

⏰ Prep: 25 minutes 🍲 Cook: 45 minutes 🍴 Serves: 4

1 (28 ounces) can of whole peeled tomatoes
¼ cup dry white wine
3 tablespoons extra-virgin olive oil
3 garlic cloves
2 strips of Lemon peel
1 sprig oregano

10 giant clams, scrubbed
½ pound raw, tail-on shrimp
½ pound dry-packed sea scallops
4 ounces feta
¼ flat-leaf parsley

1. Preheat the air fryer at 450°F/230°C on Bake mode. 2. In the ovenproof skillet over medium heat, add the wine, tomatoes, lemon peel, garlic, and oregano and cook for 20 to 25 minutes, breaking up the tomatoes and stirring occasionally. 3. Mix the clams in the tomato mixture and then transfer to the baking pan. 4. Bake them in the preheated air fryer for 15 minutes. 5. When the time is up, add the shrimps, scallops, and feta cheese. 6. Return the pan to the air fryer, and cook them for about 5 minutes longer on Broil mode at 300°F/150°C. 7. When done, serve and enjoy.

Per Serving: Calories 332; Fat 20.95g; Sodium 1210mg; Carbs 18.97g; Fiber 4.6g; Sugar 2.96g; Protein 20.67g

Flavorful Fried Scallops

🕐 Prep: 10 minutes   🍲 Cook: 15 minutes   📚 Serves: 2

⅓ cup shallots, chopped
1½ tablespoons olive oil
1½ tablespoons coconut aminos
1 tablespoon Mediterranean seasoning mix
½ tablespoon balsamic vinegar

½ teaspoon ginger, grated
1 clove of garlic, chopped
1 pound scallops, cleaned
Cooking spray

1. Heat all the ingredients except for the scallops in the skillet over medium heat for 3 minutes. 2. Transfer the mixture to a large bowl, and set it aside to cool. 3. Add the scallops, mix well and then marinate for at least 2 hours. 4. When ready, place the scallops in the baking pan in a single layer and spray with cooking spray. 5. Air Fry the food at 345°F/170°C for 10 minutes, flipping the scallops halfway through. 6. When cooking is complete, the scallops should be tender and opaque. 7. Remove from the air fryer and serve.

Per Serving: Calories 293; Fat 11.33g; Sodium 1216mg; Carbs 17.2g; Fiber 1.9g; Sugar 4.13g; Protein 28.64g

Beer Broiled White Fish Fillets

🕐 Prep: 15 minutes   🍲 Cook: 20 minutes   📚 Serves: 4

½ tablespoon vegetable oil
1 cup flour
½ teaspoons pepper
¼ teaspoon garlic salt
⅔ cup beer

2 egg whites
2 cups dry breadcrumbs
½ cup chopped parsley
1-½ pounds of white fish fillets
Cooking spray

1. Grease the baking pan with the vegetable oil. 2. Mix up the flour, pepper, garlic salt, and beer in a large bowl. 3. Beat the egg whites and gently fold them into the flour mixture. 4. Add parsley and breadcrumbs to another bowl. 5. Dip each fish fillet in the flour mixture and then dip it in the breadcrumb mixture. 6. Arrange the fillet to the prepared baking pan and then coat them with the cooking spray. 7. Bake the fillets at 450°F/230°C for 15 minutes. 8. When the time is up, cook the food on Broil mode at High for one minute longer. 9. Serve warm.

Per Serving: Calories 465; Fat 16.62g; Sodium 247mg; Carbs 55.93g; Fiber 5g; Sugar 25.49g; Protein 24.13g

Air Fried Spicy Bay Scallops

🕐 Prep: 5 minutes   🍲 Cook: 10 minutes   📚 Serves: 4

1-pound Bay scallops
2 teaspoons smoked Paprika
2 teaspoons chili powder
2 teaspoons olive oil

1 teaspoon garlic powder
¼ teaspoon ground black pepper
⅛ teaspoon cayenne red pepper

1. Mix up bay scallops with the remaining ingredients in a suitable bowl, and then transfer them to the cooking tray. 2. Air Fry them at 400°F/200°C for 8 minutes, shaking the cooking tray halfway through. 3. When done, serve and enjoy.

Per Serving: Calories 108; Fat 3.17g; Sodium 485mg; Carbs 5.59g; Fiber 1g; Sugar 0.24g; Protein 14.17g

Cheese Crab Stuffed Mushrooms

⏰ **Prep: 25 minutes**   🍲 **Cook: 15 minutes**   🍃 **Serves: 6**

1 pound mushrooms
7 ounces crab-meat
5 thinly sliced green onions
¼ teaspoon dried thyme
¼ teaspoon dried oregano
¼ teaspoon ground savory

Ground black pepper to taste
¼ cup plus 3 tablespoons grated Parmesan cheese
⅓ cup Mayonnaise
¼ teaspoon paprika

1. Mix the crab-meat with the onions, herbs pepper, mayonnaise, and ¼ cup of Parmesan cheese in a mixing bowl. 2. Place the bowl in the refrigerator and let the mixture sit until ready to use. 3. Wipe the mushrooms clean, remove stems and spoon out and discard the gills and the base of the stem, making deep cuts. 4. Fill each mushroom cap with the crab-meat mixture and sprinkle with the paprika and the remaining Parmesan cheese; arrange them to the baking pan. 5. Bake them at 350°F/175°C for 15 minutes. 6. When done, serve and enjoy.

Per Serving: Calories 182; Fat 5.64g; Sodium 148mg; Carbs 18.43g; Fiber 7g; Sugar 2.37g; Protein 17.32g

Fried Coconut Shrimp

⏰ **Prep: 15 minutes**   🍲 **Cook: 20 minutes**   🍃 **Serves: 2**

½-pound uncooked large shrimp, peeled and deveined
½ cup sweetened shredded coconut
3 tablespoons Panko breadcrumbs
2 large egg whites
Sauce:
⅓ cup apricot preserves
½ teaspoon cider vinegar

⅛ teaspoon salt
Dash of pepper
Dash of Louisiana-style hot sauce
3 tablespoons all-purpose flour

Dash of crushed red pepper flakes

1. Combine the coconut and bread crumbs in the bowl. 2. Mix up the egg whites, spicy sauce, salt, and pepper in another bowl. 3. Add the flour to the third bowl. 4. Coat the shrimp with the flour, shake off excess flour, then dip the shrimp in the egg white mixture and lastly in the coconut mixture, patting to ensure the coating sticks. 5. Grease the baking pan with oil or cooking spray; place the coated shrimp in a single layer in the pan. 6. Air Fry the shrimp at 375°F/190°C for 8 minutes, turning them halfway through. 7. Add all the sauce ingredients to the saucepan over medium-low heat and simmer them until preserves are melted. 8. Serve the shrimp with the sauce.

Per Serving: Calories 455; Fat 1.62g; Sodium 379mg; Carbs 107.46g; Fiber 12g; Sugar 76.83g; Protein 12.1g

Crispy Breaded Fish Fillets

⏰ **Prep: 15 minutes**   🍲 **Cook: 15 minutes**   🍃 **Serves: 4**

¾ cup bread crumbs or Panko or crushed cornflakes
1 packet dry ranch-style dressing mix
2½ tablespoons vegetable oil

2 eggs, beaten
4 salmon or other fish fillets
Lemon wedges to garnish

1. Add the bread crumbs and ranch dressing mix to the bowl, combine them well, and mix the oil until the mixture is loose and crumbly. 2. As you dip the fish fillets in the egg, allow the extra egg to drip off. 3. Thoroughly coat the fillets with the crumb mixture and then arrange them on the cooking tray. 4. Air Fry the fillets at 350°F/175°C for 12 minutes. 5. After cooking, you can squeeze lemon slices over them and serve.

Per Serving: Calories 312; Fat 21.66g; Sodium 158mg; Carbs 4.57g; Fiber 0.2g; Sugar 1.04g; Protein 24.09g

Savory Tuna Burgers

⏱ **Prep: 10 minutes**　🍲 **Cook: 15 minutes**　🍃 **Serves: 4**

1 large egg, lightly beaten
½ cup dry bread crumbs
½ cup finely chopped celery
⅓ cup mayonnaise
¼ cup finely chopped onion

2 tablespoons chili sauce
1 pouch (6.4 ounces) of light tuna in water
4 hamburger buns, split and toasted
Lettuce leaves and sliced tomato (optional)

1. Grease the cooking tray with oil or cooking spray. 2. Mix the tuna meat with the egg, crumbs, celery, and mayonnaise, then shape them into four patties. 3. Place the patties in a single layer on the cooking tray. 4. Air Fry the patties at 350°F/175°C for 12 minutes, flipping them halfway through. 5. When done, place one patty between two bun pieces, and you can serve.

Per Serving: Calories 304; Fat 10.27g; Sodium 716mg; Carbs 34.21g; Fiber 2.5g; Sugar 5.1g; Protein 17.89g

Crunchy Popcorn Shrimp

⏱ **Prep: 15 minutes**　🍲 **Cook: 10 minutes**　🍃 **Serves: 4**

12 ounces large shrimp, peeled and deveined
¼ cup all-purpose flour
1 egg
1 cup Panko bread crumbs
½ teaspoon paprika

½ teaspoon onion powder
¼ teaspoon salt
⅛ teaspoon ground black pepper
Nonstick cooking spray

1. Evenly coat the shrimp with flour in a large mixing bowl. 2. Beat the egg in another bowl. 3. Mix up the bread crumbs, onion powder, paprika, salt, and pepper in the third bowl. 4. Dip the shrimp in the egg, and then in the dry mixture. 5. Spray the baking pan with the nonstick cooking spray; arrange the shrimp on the baking pan. 6. Air Fry the coated shrimp at 400°F/205°C for 8 minutes, flipping and spraying any chalky spots with cooking spray halfway through. 7. When done, serve and enjoy.

Per Serving: Calories 110; Fat 2.12g; Sodium 647mg; Carbs 7.79g; Fiber 0.4g; Sugar 0.22g; Protein 13.95g

Breaded Haddock Fillets

⏱ **Prep: 10 minutes**　🍲 **Cook: 15 minutes**　🍃 **Serves: 4**

1 cup dry bread crumbs
¼ cup vegetable oil
4 haddock fillets

1 egg, beaten
1 lemon, sliced

1. Add the bread crumbs and oil to a mixing bowl, and stir them until the mixture is crumbly and loose. 2. Add the egg to another bowl. 3. Dip the fillets into the egg and evenly coat them with the bread crumb mixture. 4. Arrange the coated fillets on the cooking tray. 5. Air Fry the fillets at 350°F/175°C for 12 minutes until the haddock flakes easily with a fork. 6. When done, transfer the fillets to a plate, and you can garnish them with the lemon slices.

Per Serving: Calories 402; Fat 18.36g; Sodium 634mg; Carbs 20.52g; Fiber 1.3g; Sugar 2.14g; Protein 37.39g

Garlic Roasted Lobster Tails

⏰ **Prep: 10 minutes**　🍲 **Cook: 8 minutes**　🍃 **Serves: 2**

12 ounces lobster tails
1 tablespoon garlic, minced
2 tablespoon butter, melted

1 teaspoon fresh lemon juice
Salt

1. Mix up the butter, lemon juice, salt, and garlic in the bowl, then brush the processed lobster tails with the mixture. 2. Arrange the lobster tails in the baking pan. 3. Roast the lobster tails at 380°F/195°C for 8 minutes. 4. When done, transfer the lobster tails to the serving plate.

Per Serving: Calories 240; Fat 12.82g; Sodium 889mg; Carbs 1.59g; Fiber 0.1g; Sugar 0.12g; Protein 28.5g

Homemade Bacon Wrapped Scallops

⏰ **Prep: 15 minutes**　🍲 **Cook: 5 minutes**　🍃 **Serves: 4**

16 sea scallops
8 slices of bacon, cut into halves
8 toothpicks

Salt
Freshly ground black pepper

1. Pat dry the scallops with a paper towel. 2. Wrap the scallop with a half slice of bacon, and then secure the bacon-wrapped scallops with a toothpick. 3. Place the scallops in a baking pan in a single layer, spray the scallops with olive oil, and season them with salt and pepper. 4. Air Fry them at 370°F/185°C for 5 minutes. 5. When cooked, transfer the food to the serving bowl.

Per Serving: Calories 295; Fat 21.01g; Sodium 754mg; Carbs 4.26g; Fiber 0g; Sugar 0.43g; Protein 20.99g

Crab-Corn Patties

⏰ **Prep: 10 minutes**　🍲 **Cook: 10 minutes**　🍃 **Serves: 4**

1 egg
8 ounces crab meat, drained
½ cup breadcrumbs
½ cup mayonnaise
2 green onions, chopped

1½ cups corn kernels
2 tablespoons parsley, chopped
1 tablespoon Dijon mustard
Pepper
Salt

1. Thoroughly mix up all the ingredients in a large bowl. 2. Form the mixture into patties and then arrange them on the cooking tray. 3. Air Fry the patties at 375F/190C for 10 minutes, flipping them halfway through. 4. When done, transfer the patties to the serving plate.

Per Serving: Calories 417; Fat 15.52g; Sodium 564mg; Carbs 44.63g; Fiber 13.3g; Sugar 4.19g; Protein 29.47g

Baked Spicy Tiger Shrimp

⏰ **Prep: 15 minutes**　🍲 **Cook: 5 minutes**　🍃 **Serves: 8**

2 teaspoons old bay seasoning
1 teaspoon cayenne pepper
1 teaspoon smoked paprika

4 tablespoons olive oil
2 pounds tiger shrimp
Salt to taste

1. In the bowl, mix up all the ingredients. 2. Place the shrimp in the baking pan, then place the pan in the air fryer. 3. Bake the shrimp at 350°F/175°C for 5 minutes. 4.Serve warm.

Per Serving: Calories 158; Fat 7.42g; Sodium 155mg; Carbs 0.4g; Fiber 0.2g; Sugar 0.05g; Protein 22.87g

Simple Bacon Wrapped Shrimp

🕐 **Prep: 15 minutes** 🍲 **Cook: 10 minutes** 🍃 **Serves: 4**

1¼ pounds tiger shrimp, peeled and deveined Salt and pepper
1-pound bacon

1. Wrap shrimp with a slice of bacon. 2. Season the food with salt and pepper, then refrigerate them for 20 minutes. 3. Arrange the bacon shrimp in the baking pan. 4. Air Fry them at 350°F/175°C for 7 minutes. 5. When done, transfer the food to the serving plate.

Per Serving: Calories 477; Fat 34.24g; Sodium 1873mg; Carbs 8.28g; Fiber 3.2g; Sugar 0.8g; Protein 40.77g

Parsley Roasted Swordfish Steaks

🕐 **Prep: 10 minutes** 🍲 **Cook: 20 minutes** 🍃 **Serves: 2**

2 swordfish steaks
1 teaspoon cumin
1 tablespoon fresh lemon juice
1 tablespoon canola oil
1 teaspoon garlic, minced

¼ cup parsley, chopped
¼ teaspoon red pepper flakes, crushed
½ teaspoon paprika
Pepper
Salt

1. Mix up the oil, cumin, paprika, red pepper flakes, garlic, parsley, lemon juice, salt, and pepper in a bowl. 2. Add the swordfish steaks to the mixture and evenly coat them. 3. Arrange the swordfish steaks in the baking pan. 4. Roast the swordfish steaks at 390°F/198°C for 20 minutes, flipping them halfway through. 5. Allow the swordfish steaks to cool before serving.

Per Serving: Calories 272; Fat 16.45g; Sodium 195mg; Carbs 2.82g; Fiber 0.7g; Sugar 0.64g; Protein 27.47g

Buttered Sea Scallops

🕐 **Prep: 15 minutes** 🍲 **Cook: 5 minutes** 🍃 **Serves: 8**

4 tablespoons butter, melted
3 pounds of sea scallops

2 tablespoons fresh thyme, minced
Salt and freshly ground black pepper to taste

1. Mix the butter, thyme, salt, and pepper in the bowl, add the sea scallops and then coat them with the mixture. 2. Arrange the sea scallops in the baking pan. 3. Bake the sea scallops at 385°F/195°C for 5 minutes. 4. When done, transfer the food to the serving bowl.

Per Serving: Calories 170; Fat 6.61g; Sodium 713mg; Carbs 5.74g; Fiber 0.2g; Sugar 0.01g; Protein 20.64g

Delicious Sardine-Zucchini Patties

⏰ Prep: 15 minutes   🍲 Cook: 15 minutes   🍃 Serves: 4

½ pound zucchini, grated
12 ounces sardines, drained and chopped
4 tablespoons scallions, chopped
1 teaspoon garlic, minced

1 large egg, whisked
Red onion, minced
1 celery stick, minced
½ cup bread crumbs

1. Line the baking pan with a sheet of parchment paper. 2. In a large mixing bowl, thoroughly mix up all the ingredients. 3. Form the mixture into four patties and then place them in a single layer in the baking pan. 4. Air Fry the patties at 350°F/175°C for 12 minutes. 5. Serve warm.

Per Serving: Calories 270; Fat 11.86g; Sodium mg; Carbs 369g; Fiber 1.9g; Sugar 2.23g; Protein 25.44g

Flavorful Tuna Arugula Salad

⏰ Prep: 15 minutes   🍲 Cook: 15 minutes   🍃 Serves: 4

14 ounces canned tuna, drained and flaked
2 spring onions; chopped.
1 cup arugula

1 tablespoon olive oil
1 pinch of salt and black pepper

1. Mix all the ingredients except for the oil and arugula in a bowl, then arrange them in the baking pan. 2. Bake them at 360°F/180°C for 15 minutes. 3. When done, combine the arugula with the tuna mix in the serving bowl and enjoy.

Per Serving: Calories 169; Fat 4.49g; Sodium 260mg; Carbs 12.69g; Fiber 1.6g; Sugar 8.41g; Protein 20.74g

Sweet & Spicy Shrimp Skewers

⏰ Prep: 15 minutes   🍲 Cook: 10 minutes   🍃 Serves: 2

1 tablespoon lime juice
1 tablespoon honey
¼ teaspoon red pepper flakes
¼ teaspoon pepper
¼ teaspoon ginger
Nonstick cooking spray

1-pound medium shrimp, peel, devein and leave tails on
1 cups peas, drain and chop
½ green bell pepper, chopped fine
¼ cup scallions, chopped

1. Whisk lime juice, honey, and spices in the sauce bowl. 2. Transfer 2 tablespoons of the mixture to a medium bowl. 3. Thread 5 shrimp on a skewer, brush both sides with marinade, and place them in the baking pan. 4. Bake them at 400°F/200°C for 10 minutes. 5. While cooking the skewers, in a bowl, add the peas, bell pepper, and scallions to the reserved honey mixture, and mix well. 6. Divide salsa evenly between serving plates and top with two skewers.

Per Serving: Calories 210; Fat 2.49g; Sodium 1288mg; Carbs 14.61g; Fiber 0.8g; Sugar 10.26g; Protein 31.66g

Chapter 5 Chicken and Poultry Recipes

Garlic Chicken Meatballs

🕐 **Prep: 10 minutes** 🍲 **Cook: 15 minutes** 🍃 **Serves: 2**

½ pound chicken breast
1 tablespoon of garlic
1 tablespoon of onion

½ cup chicken broth
1 tablespoon of oatmeal or whole wheat flour

1. Add all the ingredients to the food processor, and process until they are ground and mixed well. 2. Make meatballs from the ground mixture and arrange them evenly on the cooking tray. 3. Air Fry the meatballs at 400°F/200°C for 15 minutes, shaking them several times during cooking. 4. When cooked, carefully remove it from the chicken and transfer it to a serving plate. 5. Serve and enjoy!

Per Serving: Calories 220; Fat 10.74g; Sodium 303mg; Carbs 4.84g; Fiber 0.6g; Sugar 0.54g; Protein 24.86g

Beer Roasted Chicken Thighs

🕐 **Prep: 10 minutes** 🍲 **Cook: 45 minutes** 🍃 **Serves: 4**

2 ¼ pounds of chicken thigh
½ (12-ounce) can of beer
4 cloves of garlic

1 large onion
Salt and pepper to taste

1. Evenly arrange the chicken thigh on the baking pan. 2. Add onion, garlic, salt, pepper, and beer to a blender and beat together. 3. Pour the mixture over the chicken to cover and soak. 4. Place the baking pan in the air fryer. 5. Roast them at 390°F/200°C for 45 minutes until the beer has dried a bit and a golden-brown cone appears on top. 6. When cooked, carefully remove from the air fryer and transfer to a serving plate. 7. Serve and enjoy!

Per Serving: Calories 685; Fat 50.83g; Sodium 438mg; Carbs 10.75g; Fiber 1.1g; Sugar 2.34g; Protein 43.61g

Easy Fried Turkey Tenderloin

🕐 **Prep: 10 minutes** 🍲 **Cook: 45 minutes** 🍃 **Serves: 4**

1½ pound turkey breast tenderloin
½ tablespoon olive oil
1 teaspoon Italian seasoning

¼ teaspoon pepper
½ teaspoon salt

1. Preheat the air fryer at 390°F/200°C on Bake mode. 2. Brush olive oil over the turkey and add the Italian seasoning, pepper, and salt to season. 3. Transfer the turkey to a baking dish and bake in the preheated air fryer for 45 minutes until a meat thermometer reads 165°F/75°C. 4. When cooked, carefully remove the turkey from the air fryer. 5. Serve and enjoy!

Per Serving: Calories 190; Fat 4.53g; Sodium 693mg; Carbs 0.75g; Fiber 0.1g; Sugar 0.16g; Protein 36.69g

Turkey-Mushroom Patties

⏰ Prep: 10 minutes 🍲 Cook: 20 minutes 🥙 Serves: 4

1 ounce of mushrooms; chopped
1 teaspoon garlic powder
1 teaspoon onion powder

1 ¼ pounds turkey meat; ground
Cooking spray
Salt and black pepper to the taste

1. Mix salt, pepper, and mushroom together in a blender and pulse well. 2. Then add onion powder, garlic powder, turkey, salt, and pepper and mix well. 3. Make 4 patties out from the mixture. 4. Arrange the patties evenly on the baking pan, then place the pan in the air fryer. 5. Bake the patties at 320°F/160°C for minutes. 6. When cooked, carefully remove the patties from the air fryer and transfer them to a serving plate. 7. Serve and enjoy!

Per Serving: Calories 237; Fat 10.96g; Sodium 84mg; Carbs 6.76g; Fiber 1.1g; Sugar 0.22g; Protein 28.8g

Orange-Flavored Duck Breasts

⏰ Prep: 10 minutes 🍲 Cook: 15 minutes 🥙 Serves: 4

4 (6-ounce) skin-on duck breasts
1 teaspoon salt
¼ cup orange marmalade

1 tablespoon white balsamic vinegar
¾ teaspoon ground black pepper

1. Cut on the skin of the duck breasts 10 slits. 2. Rub salt over the meat to season. 3. Arrange the breasts onto the cooking tray skin-side up, then place the tray in the air fryer. 4. Air Fry the breasts at 400°F/200°C for 10 minutes. 5. While the breasts are cooking, add all the rest ingredients to a small bowl and combine well. 6. When cooked, brush the mixture evenly over the breasts and flip to the other side. 7. Return to the air fryer and cook for 3 minutes or more, until the flesh is browned well and the skin becomes crispy. 8. Serve and enjoy!

Per Serving: Calories 106; Fat 1.82g; Sodium 618mg; Carbs 14.21g; Fiber 0.2g; Sugar 12.6g; Protein 8.56g

Peach-Flavored Chicken Wings

⏰ Prep: 10 minutes 🍲 Cook: 15 minutes 🥙 Serves: 8

½ cup peach preserves
1 tablespoon brown sugar
1 garlic clove, minced
¼ teaspoon salt
1 tablespoon white vinegar

1 tablespoon bourbon
1 teaspoon cornstarch
1½ teaspoon water
2 pounds of chicken wings

1. Heat the air fryer to 400°F/200°C. 2. In a food processor, blend together garlic, salt, and brown sugar until smooth. 3. In a saucepan, add the mixture, bourbon, peach preserves, and vinegar and bring together to a boil. 4. Then reduce heat to simmer until the mixture thickens, about 6 minutes. 5. Combine the cornstarch and water and then add the mixture into the saucepan to cook until the mixture thickens about 2 minutes. Reserve ¼ cup of the cooking liquid. 6. Arrange the wings in the cooking tray and brush the sauce mixture over. 7. Insert the cooking tray inside the air fryer. 8. Air Fry the food at 350°F/175°C for 6 minutes. 9. When cooked, flip the chicken wings to the other side and brush the other side with the sauce mixture. 10. Then fry the other side for 8 minutes. 11. When cooked, remove from the air fryer and transfer to a serving plate. 12. Serve and enjoy!

Per Serving: Calories 164; Fat 4.03g; Sodium 166mg; Carbs 4.71g; Fiber 0.2g; Sugar 4.04g; Protein 25.01g

Air Fried Chicken Breasts with Orange Sauce

⏰ **Prep: 5 minutes**   🍳 **Cook: 15 minutes**   🥘 **Serves: 2**

1 pound boneless and skinless chicken breasts

For the Orange Sauce:
½ cup orange juice
2 tablespoons brown sugar
1 teaspoon soy sauce
1 teaspoon rice wine vinegar

2 tablespoons cornstarch or potato starch

¼ teaspoon ground ginger
Dash of red pepper flakes
Zest of one orange
2 teaspoons cornstarch with 2 teaspoons water

1. Heat your air fryer to 360°F/180°C to 400°F/200°C before cooking on the Air Fry function. 2. Mix the chicken pieces with cornstarch in a mixing bowl until well coated. 3. Arrange the coated chicken on the cooking tray, and insert it into your air fryer. 4. Air Fry them at 360°F/180°C to 400°F/200°C and time to 7 to 9 minutes, depending on your favored doneness. 5. While the chicken is cooking, add soy sauce, brown sugar, rice wine vinegar, orange zest, red pepper flakes, ginger, ginger, and orange juice in a small saucepan and simmer over medium heat for about 5 minutes. 6. Combine together the cornstarch and water. Then add the mixture to the saucepan. Simmer and stir for 1 minute. 7. When cooked, carefully remove the chicken wings from the air fryer and transfer them to a serving plate. 8. Serve the crispy chicken wings with the prepared sauce. Enjoy!

Per Serving: Calories 395; Fat 6.56g; Sodium 146mg; Carbs 28.61g; Fiber 1g; Sugar 14.67g; Protein 52.19g

Crispy Chicken Thighs

⏰ **Prep: 10 minutes**   🍳 **Cook: 35 minutes**   🥘 **Serves: 4**

2 tablespoons melted butter
1 cup crushed cornflakes
1 cup all-purpose flour
1-½ teaspoons seasoned salt

4 chicken drumsticks
4 bone-in chicken thighs
¾ cup apple sauce

1. Preheat your air fryer to 360°F/180°C to 425°F/220°C on the Bake function. 2. Add the seasoned salt, cornflakes, and flour to a shallow bowl and combine well. 3. Add applesauce to a separate shallow dish. 4. Dredge the chicken in the applesauce and then in the cornflake mixture until the chicken drumsticks are well coated. 5. Arrange the chicken drumsticks onto the baking pan, meatier side down, and then insert the baking pan inside the air fryer. 6. Bake them for 20 minutes, then flip to the other and bake for 10 to 15 minutes or more. 7. When the cooking has finished, carefully remove the baked chicken and transfer it to a serving plate. 8. Serve and enjoy!

Per Serving: Calories 737; Fat 43.03g; Sodium 1197mg; Carbs 32.05g; Fiber 2.9g; Sugar 4.67g; Protein 53.15g

Crunchy Chicken Schnitzel

⏰ **Prep: 15 minutes**   🍳 **Cook: 10 minutes**   🥘 **Serves: 4**

1 pound skinless, boneless chicken thighs
½ cup seasoned bread crumbs
1 teaspoon salt
½ teaspoon ground black pepper

¼ cup flour
1 egg, beaten
Avocado oil cooking spray

1. Flatten the chicken thighs between two sheets of parchment paper with a mallet. 2. Add bread crumbs, salt, and black pepper to a shallow dish and combine well. 3. In a second bowl, add the flour. 4. In a third bowl, add the beaten egg. 5. Before cooking, heat your air fryer to 360°F/180°C to 375°F/190°C on the Air Fry function. 6. Dip the chicken thighs first in the flour, then in egg, and finally in the bread crumbs, pressing to coat well. 7. Arrange the coated chicken thighs onto the cooking tray and spritz with olive oil. 8. Air Fry them at 360°F/180°C to 375°F/190°C for 6 minutes. 9. When the cooking time is done, flip to the other side and mist with oil. 10. Cook again for 3 to 4 minutes. 11. Carefully remove from the air fryer and transfer to a serving bowl. 12. Serve and enjoy!

Per Serving: Calories 266; Fat 9.04g; Sodium 741mg; Carbs 9.12g; Fiber 0.4g; Sugar 0.78g; Protein 34.45g

Roasted Cornish Hen

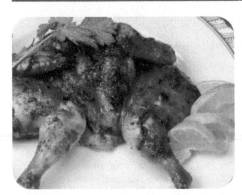

⏰ Prep: 5 minutes   🍲 Cook: 45 minutes   🍥 Serves: 2

2 Cornish hens
2 tablespoons olive oil
2 teaspoons salt
1-½ teaspoons Italian seasoning

1 teaspoon garlic powder
1 teaspoon paprika
½ teaspoon black pepper
½ teaspoon lemon zest

1. Preheat the air fryer to 360°F/180°C on Roast function. 2. Mix oil, black pepper, paprika, salt, lemon zest, garlic powder, and Italian seasoning in a small bowl. 3. Dry the Cornish hens and brush the seasoning mixture over the hens. 4. Arrange the seasoned hens onto the cooking tray and then insert them inside the air fryer. 5. Cook them on Roast function at 360°F/180°C for 35 minutes. 6. When the cooking time is up, flip to the other side and cook for 10 minutes. 7. Carefully remove the chicken from the air fryer. 8. Serve and enjoy!

Per Serving: Calories 412; Fat 21.68g; Sodium 2566mg; Carbs 2.92g; Fiber 0.9g; Sugar 0.31g; Protein 48.64g

Cheese Chicken Taquitos

⏰ Prep: 15 minutes   🍲 Cook: 20 minutes   🍥 Serves: 6

1 teaspoon vegetable oil
2 tablespoons diced onion
1 clove of garlic, minced
2 tablespoons chopped green chilies
2 tablespoons Mexican-style hot tomato sauce
1 cup shredded rotisserie chicken

2 tablespoons Neufchatel cheese
½ cup shredded Mexican cheese blend
1 pinch salt and ground black pepper
6 each corn tortillas
1 serving avocado oil cooking spray

1. Preheat the air fryer 360°F/180°C to 400°F/200°C on the Air Fry function. 2. Heat 1 teaspoon vegetable oil in a skillet. When heated, add onion and cook for 3 to 5 minutes. 3. Then add garlic and cook for 1 minute. 4. Stir in Mexican tomato sauce and green chilies until well combined. 5. Add Mexican cheese blend, Mexican tomato sauce, and chicken to the skillet and cook for about 3 minutes. 6. Add salt and pepper to season. 7. Heat the tortilla in the skillet until the tortilla is soft. 8. In the center of each tortilla, add 3 tablespoons of chicken mixture. Then fold and roll into taquitos. 9. On the cooking tray, evenly arrange the tortillas and then insert them into the preheated air fryer. 10. Spritz the tortilla with avocado oil. 11. Air Fry them for 6 to 9 minutes. 12. When the cooking time is up, flip once and cook again for 3 to 5 minutes. 13. When cooked, carefully remove from the air fryer and transfer to a serving plate. 14. Serve and enjoy!

Per Serving: Calories 156; Fat 5.87g; Sodium 171mg; Carbs 12.92g; Fiber 1.8g; Sugar 1.23g; Protein 13.1g

Thai-Style Chicken Kabobs

⏰ Prep: 10 minutes   🍲 Cook: 15 minutes   🍥 Serves: 4

2 pounds of skinless chicken breasts
½ cup Tamari soy sauce
¼ cup coconut milk

3 tablespoons lime juice
3 tablespoons maple syrup
1-2 tablespoons Thai red curry

1. Soak the bamboo skewers for about 30 minutes. 2. Add Thai red curry paste, coconut milk, tamari soy sauce, and coconut oil in a mixing bowl and mix well. 3. Add the chicken to the bowl and set aside to marinate for at least 2 hours. 4. Thread the marinated chicken onto the skewers. 5. Arrange the chicken skewers onto the cooking tray, and insert them in the preheated air fryer. 6. Roast the skewers at 350°F/175°C for 12 to 15 minutes. 7. When cooked, carefully remove from the air fryer and transfer to a serving plate. 8. Serve and enjoy!

Per Serving: Calories 355; Fat 10.75g; Sodium 2424mg; Carbs 15.51g; Fiber 0.9g; Sugar 10.72g; Protein 50.89g

Crisp Chicken Tenderloins

🕐 Prep: 15 minutes   🍲 Cook: 15 minutes   🌿 Serves: 4

1 egg
½ cup dry bread crumbs

2 tablespoons vegetable oil
8 chicken tenderloins

1. Preheat the air fryer to 350°F/175°C on the Air Fry function. 2. Beat an egg in a small bowl. 3. Add oil and the bread crumbs to a separate bowl and combine well. 4. First, dip the chicken in the egg, and then evenly coat the bread crumbs. 5. Arrange them evenly on the cooking tray and cook in the preheated air fryer for 12 minutes. 6. When cooked, carefully remove from the air fryer and transfer to a serving plate. 7. Serve and enjoy!

Per Serving: Calories 349; Fat 23.68g; Sodium 233mg; Carbs 10.15g; Fiber 0.6g; Sugar 1.06g; Protein 22.27g

Tasty Orange Chicken

🕐 Prep: 5 minutes   🍲 Cook: 15 minutes   🌿 Serves: 4

2 pounds boneless skinless chicken breasts or chicken thighs
For the Orange Sauce
1 cup orange juice
4 tablespoons brown sugar
2 tablespoons soy sauce
2 tablespoons rice wine vinegar
½ teaspoon ground ginger (or ½ teaspoon
Optional to Serve
Green onions, chopped

4 tablespoons corn starch or potato starch

freshly grated ginger)
A dash of red pepper flakes
Zest of one orange
4 teaspoons corn-starch mixed with 2 teaspoons water

Sesame seeds

1. Toss together the chicken pieces with the corn-starch in a mixing bowl and stir well to coat. 2. Arrange them onto the cooking tray and insert inside the preheated air fryer on Position 4. 3. Cook the chicken pieces at 400°F/200°C for 7 to 9 minutes until the internal meat thermometer reads 165°F/74°C, shaking halfway through cooking. 4. In a small saucepan, add orange juice, rice wine vinegar, soy sauce, red pepper flakes, orange zest, ginger, and brown sugar and heat over medium heat. 5. Bring together to a low boil and let it boil for 5 minutes. 6. Add corn-starch and water to a separate bowl and stir into the orange sauce. Simmer for 1 more minute and stir. Turn off the heat. 7. When the chicken has completely cooked, carefully remove it from the air fryer. Add the orange juice sauce mixture to the chicken and combine well. 8. Add sesame seeds and green onions on top to garnish, as you desire. 9. Serve and enjoy!

Per Serving: Calories 412; Fat 8.48g; Sodium 233mg; Carbs 27.58g; Fiber 1.9g; Sugar 15.88g; Protein 53.58g

BBQ Chicken Drumsticks

🕐 Prep: 5 minutes   🍲 Cook: 25 minutes   🌿 Serves: 5

5-6 chicken drumsticks
⅛ cup extra virgin olive oil
½ teaspoon garlic powder
¼ teaspoon paprika
¼ teaspoon onion powder

¼ teaspoon salt
⅛ teaspoon pepper
½ cup BBQ sauce
Pinch of cayenne pepper to add spice (optional)

1. Mix the garlic powder, paprika, onion powder, cayenne pepper, salt, and olive oil in a bowl. 2. Add the chicken to the mixture and massage for a few minutes to season well. 3. Arrange the chicken drumsticks evenly in the cooking tray and insert them inside the preheated air fryer. 4. Air Fry the chicken drumsticks at 400°F/200°C for 20 minutes; after 15 minutes of cooking time, flip to the other side and cook for 5 minutes. 5. Brush both sides with BBQ sauce and continue cooking until the internal meat temperature reaches 165°F/74°C for about 3 to 5 minutes. 6. When the chicken is completely cooked, carefully remove it from the air fryer. 7. Serve with more BBQ sauce as desired. Enjoy!

Per Serving: Calories 262; Fat 15.64g; Sodium 500mg; Carbs 2.41g; Fiber 0.6g; Sugar 1.11g; Protein 26.38g

Palatable Korean-style Fried Chicken Thighs

⏰ Prep: 15 minutes　🍲 Cook: 15 minutes　🍽 Serves: 6

1½ pounds boneless, skinless chicken thighs, cut into bite-size pieces
2 tablespoons rice vinegar
1 tablespoon soy sauce
2 teaspoons minced fresh ginger
¾ teaspoon kosher salt
½ teaspoon freshly ground black pepper
2 large eggs, beaten
1 cup corn-starch

For The Sauce
3 tablespoons ketchup
3 tablespoons gochujang
3 tablespoons honey
2 tablespoons soy sauce
1 tablespoon sesame oil
2 garlic cloves, minced
4 scallions, thinly sliced
Toasted sesame seeds

1. Line the cooking tray with parchment paper. 2. Mix salt, pepper, soy sauce, vinegar, chicken, and ginger in a medium bowl. Let it sit for about 15 to 20 minutes to marinade. 3. Whisk the eggs in a small bowl. 4. Add the corn-starch to a separate shallow bowl. 5. Dip the chicken in the whisked egg first, and then coat in the corn-starch. 6. Arrange the chicken pieces in the cooking tray and brush with cooking oil. 7. Air Fry them at 400°F/200°C for 15 minutes, flipping them and brushing them with cooking oil halfway through. 8. Meanwhile, add ketchup, gochujang paste, soy sauce, sesame oil, garlic, and honey to a small bowl and stir well. 9. When the chicken is completely cooked, carefully remove it from the air fryer and transfer it to a medium bowl. Drizzle the sauce and toss well. 10. Top with sesame seeds and scallions, as you desire. 11. Serve and enjoy!

Per Serving: Calories 350; Fat 11.12g; Sodium 814mg; Carbs 36.29g; Fiber 3g; Sugar 13.24g; Protein 27.53g

Aromatic Szechuan Chicken Wings

⏰ Prep: 5 minutes　🍲 Cook: 30 minutes　🍽 Serves: 8

Wings:
2 pounds chicken wings, tip removed
½ teaspoon kosher salt
¼ teaspoon black pepper, freshly ground
Szechuan Sauce:
2 tablespoons sugar
¼ cup low sodium soy sauce
2 tablespoons garlic, minced
2 tablespoons Hoisin sauce
2 tablespoons oyster sauce
1 tablespoon sesame oil
¼ teaspoon salt
¼ teaspoon black pepper, freshly ground
Garnish:
1 tablespoon toasted sesame seeds

1. Trim the wings, then clean and pat them dry. Toss with salt and pepper to season. 2.Arrange the wings evenly on the cooking tray. Insert the cooking tray inside the preheated air fryer. 3. Air Fry the wings at 375°F/190°C for 25 minutes, tossing or flipping them after 15 minutes of cooking time. 4. While the wings are cooking, add all the sauce ingredients to a mixing bowl or jar and mix well to make the sauce. 5. When the cooking time is up, transfer the wings into a large mixing bowl and add the Szechuan sauce. Shake together to coat well. 6. Adjust the cooking temperature to 400°F/200°C and time to 5 minutes. 7. Air fry them in the air fryer for 5 minutes. 8. When the wings are done, carefully remove them from the air fryer and transfer them to the mixing bowl. 9. Top with sesame seeds. Serve and enjoy!

Per Serving: Calories 191; Fat 6.38g; Sodium 791mg; Carbs 5.77g; Fiber 0.4g; Sugar 3.11g; Protein 26.15g

Air Fried Chicken Fajitas

⏰ Prep: 10 minutes　🍲 Cook: 10 minutes　🍽 Serves: 4

½ pound boneless and skinless chicken breasts, cut into ½-inch wide strips
1 large red or yellow bell pepper, cut into strips
1 medium red onion, cut into strips
Optional
Pinch of cayenne pepper

1 tablespoon Mazola corn oil
1 tablespoon chilli powder
2 teaspoons lime juice
1 teaspoon cumin
Salt and pepper to taste

Tortillas for serving

1. Add the bell pepper, chicken strips, Mazola corn oil, lime juice, cumin, salt, pepper, and chilli powder in a mixing bowl and mix to combine well. 2. Air Fry them at 370°F/190°C for 10 to 13 minutes, flipping them halfway through. When the chicken has done, the internal thermometer should read 165°F/74°C at the thickest point. 3. Carefully remove from the air fryer and transfer to a serving plate. 4. Serve with warm tortillas, as you desire. Enjoy!

Per Serving: Calories 132; Fat 5.27g; Sodium 30mg; Carbs 7.68g; Fiber 1.4g; Sugar 1.34g; Protein 13.87g

Yogurt-Marinated Chicken Drumsticks

🕙 **Prep:** 10 minutes   🍳 **Cook:** 15 minutes   🍴 **Serves:** 4

6 chicken drumsticks
⅓ cup plain yogurt
1 tablespoon ginger paste
1 tablespoon garlic paste
1 tablespoon Kashmiri red chilli powder or any other mild red chilli powder

½ teaspoon ground turmeric
1 teaspoon Garam masala
1½ teaspoons kosher salt
1 tablespoon dried fenugreek leaves
1 tablespoon lemon juice
Cooking oil spray

1.Pat dry the chicken drumsticks with paper towels and remove the skin from the thickest part. 2. Slice 3 to 4 slits in their thick part. 3. Mix ginger, garlic, red chilli powder, Garam masala, salt, yogurt, and turmeric in a large bowl. 4. Gently layer the dried fenugreek leaves in the palms of your hands and rub them together to smash. 5. Add the smashed leaves to the chicken and toss. 6. Add lemon juice and mix them together until the chicken is coated well. Place the chicken drumsticks in the yogurt mixture and toss to coat. Let it sit to marinate for at least 1 hour. 7. Evenly arrange the chicken onto the cooking tray and insert it inside the preheated air fryer. 8.Air Fry them at 350°F/175°C for 15 minutes, shaking the tray and lightly spraying them with oil halfway through. 9.When the cooking time is up, the internal temperature of the thickest part should reach 165°F/75°C. 10. Cook for 1 to 2 minutes or more for charred marks but not overcook as you desire. 11. Carefully remove from the air fryer and transfer to a serving plate. 12. Serve and enjoy!

Per Serving: Calories 351; Fat 19.17g; Sodium 1154mg; Carbs 6g; Fiber 1.7g; Sugar 1.4g; Protein 37.31g

Lemony Cheese Chicken Wings

🕙 **Prep:** 10 minutes   🍳 **Cook:** 20 minutes   🍴 **Serves:** 4

12 chicken wings
1 teaspoon garlic salt
½ lemon juice

½ cup Parmesan cheese, grated
½ stick butter, melted

1. Add the melted butter, lemon juice, garlic salt, grated cheese, and chicken wings to a bowl and toss well. 2. Transfer the chicken wings into the cooking tray and insert the cooking tray inside the air fryer. 3. Air Fry the wings at 350°F/175°C for 20 minutes, flipping them once halfway through cooking. 4. Carefully remove the wings from the air fryer and transfer to a serving plate. 5. Serve and enjoy!

Per Serving: Calories 173; Fat 7.54g; Sodium 297mg; Carbs 2.38g; Fiber 0g; Sugar 0.17g; Protein 22.79g

Herb-Butter Roasted Turkey Breast

🕙 **Prep:** 10 minutes   🍳 **Cook:** 60 minutes   🍴 **Serves:** 8

2 pounds turkey breast, bone-in & skin-on
½ teaspoon fresh thyme, chopped
1 tablespoon butter, melted

½ teaspoon fresh sage, chopped
¼ teaspoon pepper
1 teaspoon salt

1. Add butter, sage, thyme, salt, and pepper to a small bowl and mix well. 2. Rub the mixture over the turkey breast. 3. Roast the breast at 325°F/165°C and time to 30 minutes, flipping halfway through. 4. Serve and enjoy!

Per Serving: Calories 191; Fat 9.41g; Sodium 369mg; Carbs 0.09g; Fiber 0g; Sugar 0g; Protein 24.85g

Simple Baked Cornish Hen

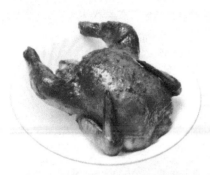

⏱ **Prep: 10 minutes** 🍲 **Cook: 25 minutes** 🍃 **Serves: 2**

1 pound Cornish hen
1 teaspoon paprika
1 tablespoon canola oil

¼ teaspoon ground black pepper
Salt

1. Lightly brush the Cornish hen with canola oil. 2. Rub over the Cornish hen with pepper, salt, and paprika to season. 3. Arrange the hen on the cooking tray, and place the tray in the air fryer. 4. Bake the hen at 390°F/200°C for 25 minutes, turning it to the other side halfway through cooking. 5. When the cooking time is up, carefully remove it from the air fryer. 6. Serve and enjoy!

Per Serving: Calories 329; Fat 14.71g; Sodium 233mg; Carbs 0.81g; Fiber 0.5g; Sugar 0.12g; Protein 45.64g

Bourbon-Flavored Chicken Wings

⏱ **Prep: 10 minutes** 🍲 **Cook: 35 minutes** 🍃 **Serves: 6**

3 pounds of chicken wings
½ cup bourbon

1 tablespoon hot chili sauce
½ cup maple syrup

1. Add chicken wings to a bowl and drizzle with hot maple syrup, bourbon, and chili sauce. Toss together. 2. Cover the bowl with plastic wrap and then place it in your refrigerator for 4 hours. 3. Arrange the chicken wings evenly onto the cooking tray, then place the tray in the air fryer. 4. Roast the chicken wings at 350°F/175°C for 35 minutes, turning them twice or more during cooking. 5. Serve and enjoy!

Per Serving: Calories 374; Fat 8.05g; Sodium 228mg; Carbs 18.17g; Fiber 0.2g; Sugar 16.17g; Protein 49.91g

Chapter 6 Beef, Pork, and Lamb Recipes

Aromatic Tomato Beef Casserole

⏰ Prep: 10 minutes   🍲 Cook: 1 hour 30 minutes   🍽 Serves: 6

1-pound lean stew beef, cut into chunks
¼ teaspoon garlic powder
1 tablespoon tomato puree
2 cups beef stock
2 tablespoons olive oil

2 teaspoons herb de Provence
3 teaspoons paprika
4 ounces of black olives, sliced
7 ounces tomatoes, chopped

1. Heat the olive oil in the pan over medium heat; add the beef chunks and cook them until brown. 2. Add the stock, olives, tomatoes, tomato puree, garlic powder, herb de Provence, and paprika, stir them well, and then boil. 3. Transfer the mixture to baking pan. 4. Bake the food at 350°F/175°C for 90 minutes. 5. When done, you can serve with hot rice.

Per Serving: Calories 177; Fat 10.81g; Sodium 656mg; Carbs 3.16g; Fiber 1.5g; Sugar 1.22g; Protein 18.18g

Cheese Beef Meatballs

⏰ Prep: 10 minutes   🍲 Cook: 20 minutes   🍽 Serves: 4

1-pound ground beef
½ small onion, chopped
1 egg, lightly beaten
2 garlic cloves, minced
1 tablespoon basil, chopped
¼ cup Parmesan cheese, grated

½ cup bread crumbs
1 tablespoon Italian parsley, chopped
1 tablespoon rosemary, chopped
2 tablespoons milk
Salt and pepper to taste

1. Mix up all the ingredients in a large bowl. 2. Form the balls from the meat mixture. 3. Bake the meatballs at 375°F/190°C for 20 minutes. 4. When done, serve and enjoy.

Per Serving: Calories 342; Fat 19.3g; Sodium 373mg; Carbs 13.93g; Fiber 1.1g; Sugar 2.57g; Protein 28.2g

Fried Rosemary-Garlic Veal Loin

⏰ Prep: 10 minutes   🍲 Cook: 12 minutes   🍽 Serves: 3

1½ teaspoons crushed fennel seeds
1 tablespoon minced fresh rosemary leaves
1 tablespoon minced garlic
1½ teaspoons lemon zest
1½ teaspoons salt

½ teaspoon red pepper flakes
2 tablespoons olive oil
3 (10-ounce) bone-in veal loin, about ½ inch thick

1. Mix up all the ingredients except for the veal loin in a large bowl. 2. Coat the veal loin with the mixture. 3. Cover the bowl with the plastic wrap and place the bowl in the refrigerator for at least 1 hour to marinate. 4. Arrange the marinated veal loin on the cooking tray. 5. Air Fry the food at 400°F/200°C for 12 minutes. 6. Flip the veal loin halfway through. 7. When done, the internal temperature of the veal should reach at least 145°F/62°C. 8. Serve immediately.

Per Serving: Calories 207; Fat 13.44g; Sodium 1258mg; Carbs 2.46g; Fiber 0.7g; Sugar 0.47g; Protein 19.77g

Classic Beef Enchiladas

⏰ Prep: 20 minutes   🍲 Cook: 5 minutes   ❦ Serves: 8

1-pound ground beef
1 package of taco seasoning
8 flour tortillas
1 can of black beans
1 can of diced tomatoes

1 can mild chopped green chilies
1 can of red enchilada sauce
1 cup shredded Mexican cheese
1 cup chopped fresh cilantro

1. Brown the ground beef in the skillet, then add the taco seasoning. 2. Place the flour tortillas on the work surface, add the beef, tomatoes, beans, and chilies to them; roll up and build the tortillas. 3. Arrange the tortillas in the baking pan and top them with the cheese. 4. Air Fry the tortillas at 355°F/180°C for 5 minutes. 5. When done, garnish with the fresh cilantro and serve.

Per Serving: Calories 327; Fat 13.68g; Sodium 623mg; Carbs 27g; Fiber 2.2g; Sugar 3.13g; Protein 22.65g

Pork Chop & Mashed Potato Casserole

⏰ Prep: 40 minutes   🍲 Cook: 40 minutes   ❦ Serves: 4

Creamy butter mashed potatoes, about 4.7 ounces
2 ounces cream cheese
2 tablespoons chopped fresh Italian parsley
3 teaspoons chopped fresh thyme leaves
3 tablespoons butter
4 boneless pork loin chops

¾ teaspoon salt, divided
¼ teaspoon pepper
2 medium onions
8 ounces Cremini mushrooms
1 cup chicken broth
1 teaspoon Worcestershire sauce
4 teaspoons all-purpose flour

1. Grease the baking pan with the cooking spray. 2. Mix up the mashed potatoes with the cream cheese, two teaspoons of thyme, and one tablespoon of parsley in a large bowl. Spoon the mixture into the baking pan and then set aside. 3. Season the pork loin chops with ½ of teaspoon salt and pepper. 4. Melt the butter in the skillet over medium heat; add the pork loin chops and cook for 1 to 2 minutes on each side, then arrange the pork loin chops in the baking pan. 5. Still in the skillet, add one tablespoon of butter, ¼ of teaspoon salt, one teaspoon of thyme, and onions, and sauté them for 7 to 8 minutes; stir in mushrooms, and sauté for 4 to 5 minutes longer. 6. Mix up Worcestershire sauce, chicken broth, and flour in the bowl, and then pour the mixture into the skillet; cook for 3 to 5 minutes. Spoon the mixture over the pork chops in the baking pan. 7. Bake the food at 400°F/200°C for 25 minutes. 8. When done, serve and enjoy.

Per Serving: Calories 464; Fat 22.38g; Sodium 942mg; Carbs 18.59g; Fiber 3g; Sugar 4.54g; Protein 46.54g

Roasted Garlic Lamb Leg

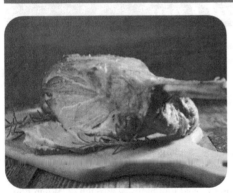

⏰ Prep: 10 minutes   🍲 Cook: 15 minutes   ❦ Serves: 4

2.5 pounds lamb leg roast
3 garlic cloves, sliced
1 tablespoon olive oil

1 tablespoon dried rosemary
Salt and pepper to taste

1. Make small slits on the meat, and then stuff the garlic slices into the slits. 2. Season the meat with salt and pepper, and rub the meat with the oil and rosemary. 3. Arrange the meat in the cooking tray. 4. Air Fry the meat at 400°F/200°C for 15 minutes. 5. When cooked, serve and enjoy.

Per Serving: Calories 554; Fat 24.04g; Sodium 197mg; Carbs 1.9g; Fiber 0.3g; Sugar 0.6g; Protein 77.44g

Easy Meatloaf with Ketchup

🕙 **Prep: 10 minutes**　　🍲 **Cook: 30 minutes**　　🍃 **Serves: 6**

Meatloaf:
2 pounds of ground beef
2 eggs, beaten
2 cups old-fashioned oats
Sauce:
1 cup ketchup
¾ cup brown sugar
¼ cup chopped onion

½ cup evaporated milk
½ cup chopped onion
½ teaspoon garlic salt

½ teaspoon liquid smoke
¼ teaspoon garlic powder
olive oil cooking spray

1. Spray the foil sheet with the cooking spray. 2. Mix up all the meatloaf ingredients in a large bowl. 3. Form the mixture into meatloaf, and then place it on the foil. 4. Roll it up a bit on the sides and place it in the cooking tray. 5. Roast them at 390°F/200°C for 20 minutes. 6. While roasting the meatloaf, whisk together all the sauce ingredients in a small saucepan over medium heat. 7. When the sauce is cooked, let cool for 1 to 2 minutes. 8. Take the meatloaf out, brush it with the sauce, and then roast them in the air fryer for 2 to 5 minutes.

Per Serving: Calories 582; Fat 26.09g; Sodium 538mg; Carbs 61.54g; Fiber 5.2g; Sugar 37.52g; Protein 39.34g

Beef & Caramelized Onion Cheeseburgers

🕙 **Prep: 50 minutes**　　🍲 **Cook: 60 minutes**　　🍃 **Serves: 6**

11 ounces refrigerated bread or original french bread
2 tablespoons butter or margarine
1 red onion, sliced, separated into rings
1 tablespoon packed brown sugar

1 tablespoon water
¼ cup Dijon mustard
1 pound thinly sliced cooked roast beef
10 slices Provolone cheese

1. Grease the baking pan with cooking spray, place the prepared bread slices on the pan, and cut side up. 2. Roast the bread at 350°F/175°C for 25 to 30 minutes, and then let them cool for 20 minutes. 3. While roasting the bread, melt the butter in the skillet over medium heat; add the onion and brown sugar, and sauté them for 10 minutes. 4. Add the water, reduce the heat to medium-low and then cook them for 10 to 15 minutes. 5. When the bread is cooled, spread mustard over them and top them with the onions, roast beef, and cheese. 6. Arrange them in the baking pan. 7. Broil them at 400°F/200°C for 3 minutes. 8. When the time is up, serve and enjoy.

Per Serving: Calories 480; Fat 21.17g; Sodium 1867mg; Carbs 33.06g; Fiber 1.8g; Sugar 4.65g; Protein 38.23g

Buttered Garlicky Steaks

🕙 **Prep: 2 hours**　　🍲 **Cook: 20 minutes**　　🍃 **Serves: 2**

2 Sirloin steaks or Rib-eyes
2 tablespoons unsalted butter
1 clove of garlic, crushed

½ teaspoon dried parsley
½ teaspoon dried rosemary
Salt and pepper

1. Sprinkle the salt and black pepper over the steaks, and let them sit for about 2 hours. 2. After 2 hours of marinating time, transfer the stakes to the cooking tray. 3. Roast the steaks at 400°F/200°C for 20 minutes, flipping them halfway through cooking. 4. While roasting the steaks, in a bowl, add the crushed garlic, butter, parsley, and rosemary; when the butter is softened, whip them together. 5. When done, prepare two foil sheets and place one steak on each. 6. Add half of the butter on top of each steak and seal the foil to 'tent' the steaks. 7. Let the steaks sit for 5 minutes before serving.

Per Serving: Calories 645; Fat 36.82g; Sodium 288mg; Carbs 2.79g; Fiber 0.5g; Sugar 1.62g; Protein 76.58g

Roasted Tomahawk Steaks

⏰ **Prep:** 10 minutes   🍲 **Cook:** 40 minutes   🍂 **Serves:** 2

2 Tomahawk steaks   Olive oil
Freshly ground black pepper   Coarse salt

1. Evenly rub the steaks with olive oil and then season them with salt and black pepper. If you use frozen tomahawk steaks, let the steaks sit at room temperature for about 30 minutes first. 2. Arrange the steaks on the cooking tray in the air fryer. 3. Roast the steaks at 375°F/190°C for 8 minutes, flipping them halfway through cooking. 4. When cooked, transfer the steaks to the cutting board, gently tent them with foil and let them rest for 10 to 15 minutes before serving.

Per Serving: Calories 412; Fat 22.55g; Sodium 683mg; Carbs 18.92g; Fiber 1g; Sugar 0.14g; Protein 33.68g

The Best Shepherd's Pie

⏰ **Prep:** 20 minutes   🍲 **Cook:** 50 minutes   🍂 **Serves:** 6

For Meat Filling
2 tablespoons olive oil
1 cup yellow onion, chopped
1-pound 90% lean ground beef
2 teaspoons dried parsley leaves
1 teaspoon dried rosemary leaves
1 teaspoon dried thyme leaves
½ teaspoon salt
½ teaspoon ground black pepper

1 tablespoon Worcestershire sauce
2 garlic cloves, minced
2 tablespoons all-purpose flour
2 tablespoons tomato paste
1 cup beef broth
1 cup frozen mixed peas and carrots
½ cup frozen corn kernels

For Potato Topping
2 pounds of russet potatoes, peeled and cut into 1-inch cubes
8 tablespoons unsalted butter

½ teaspoon garlic powder
½ teaspoon salt
¼ teaspoon ground black pepper

¼ cup Parmesan cheese

To Make the Meat Filling: 1. Heat the oil for 2 minutes in the skillet over medium-high heat; add the onions and sauté for 5 minutes. 2. Add the ground beef, parsley, rosemary, thyme, salt, and pepper to the skillet and sauté for 8 minutes, breaking the meat apart. 3. When the meat is browned, add the Worcestershire sauce and garlic and cook for 1 minute. 4. Put the flour and tomato paste, stir them until well incorporated, and no clumps of tomato paste remain. 5. Pour in the broth, and add the frozen corns, frozen peas, and carrots; when boiled, reduce the heat and simmer the food for 5 minutes, stirring occasionally. 6. When done, transfer the filling to the baking pan. 7. Bake the filling at 400°F/200°C for 10 minutes.
To Make the Topping: 1. While baking the filling, place the potatoes in a large pot and pour the water to cover the potatoes. 2. Bring the water to a boil, then reduce the heat, and simmer the potatoes for 10 to 15 minutes or until they are fork-tender. 3. Drain the potatoes in a colander and return the potatoes to the hotpot. Let the potatoes rest in the hotpot for 1 minute to evaporate any remaining liquid. 4. Add the butter, garlic powder, salt, and pepper to the pot, mash the potatoes and stir them until well combined. 5. Add the Parmesan cheese and stir well with the mashed potatoes.
Assemble the casserole: 1. In the baking pan, spread the meat mixture out into an even layer and then spoon the mashed potatoes on top of the meat. Carefully spread into an even layer. 2. Bake the dish at 400°F/200°C for 15 minutes. 3. Serve warm.

Per Serving: Calories 500; Fat 26.43g; Sodium 707mg; Carbs 38.51g; Fiber 3.7g; Sugar 3.22g; Protein 27.59g

Easy-to-Make Greek Meatballs

⏰ **Prep:** 20 minutes   🍲 **Cook:** 20 minutes   🍂 **Serves:** 6

1 pound of ground beef
¼ pound ground pork
Grated red onion, about 1 cup
2 garlic cloves
1 cup panko bread crumbs
1 egg
¼ cup finely chopped fresh parsley

1 tablespoon extra-virgin olive oil
2 teaspoons chopped mint
1 teaspoon dried oregano
½ teaspoon ground cumin
1 teaspoon salt
¼ teaspoon ground black pepper

1. Thoroughly mix up all the ingredients in the bowl. 2. Form the meatballs from the mixture. 3. Line the baking pan with the foil and spray it with cooking spray. 4. Bake the mixture at 350°F/175°C for 20 minutes. 5. When done, serve warm.

Per Serving: Calories 435; Fat 20.4g; Sodium 539mg; Carbs 8.08g; Fiber 0.9g; Sugar 3.35g; Protein 27.08g

Herbed Garlic Lamb chops

⏰ Prep: 40 minutes　🍲 Cook: 15 minutes　🍃 Serves: 8

6 tablespoons olive oil
1 tablespoon lemon juice
6 crushed garlic cloves
1 tablespoon chopped rosemary
1 tablespoons thyme

1 teaspoon dried oregano
2 teaspoons sea salt
½ teaspoon black pepper
8 large lamb chops (3.5 pounds)

1. Mix up the garlic, lemon juice, oregano, thyme, rosemary, salt, black pepper, and 3 tablespoons of olive oil in the bowl. 2. Coat the lamb chops with the garlic marinade, and then let the lamb chops stay in the marinade. 3. Cover the bowl with plastic and let the lamb chops marinate for 30 to 60 minutes at room temperature. 4. In the skillet over medium heat, heat one tablespoon of olive oil for about 2 minutes; add the marinated lamb chops and sear for 2 minutes on each side. 5. Transfer the lamb chops to the baking pan in the air fryer. 6. Roast the lamb chops at 375°F/190°C for 5 minutes. 7. Serve warm.

Per Serving: Calories 376; Fat 23.82g; Sodium 735mg; Carbs 1.2g; Fiber 0.2g; Sugar 0.08g; Protein 39.85g

Beef & Rice Stuffed Peppers

⏰ Prep: 25 minutes　🍲 Cook: 75 minutes　🍃 Serves: 2

½ cup white rice
½ cup beef flavored broth
2 large red or yellow bell peppers
½ pound lean ground beef
2 green onions, thinly sliced
½ cup shredded carrots

3 tablespoons packed brown sugar
2 tablespoons soy sauce
1 tablespoon chile-garlic sauce
½ teaspoon ground ginger
½ cup shredded Mozzarella cheese

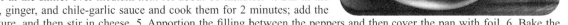

1. Cut the bell peppers in half vertically, remove the seeds and membrane, place them in the baking pan, and cut side up. 2. Mix the rice with the broth in a bowl. 3. Sauté the green onion whites, carrots, and beef in the skillet over medium heat for about 10 minutes. 4. Stir in the soy sauce, brown sugar, ginger, and chile-garlic sauce and cook them for 2 minutes; add the mixture to the rice mixture, and then stir in cheese. 5. Apportion the filling between the peppers and then cover the pan with foil. 6. Bake the dish at 425°F/220°C for 50 minutes. 7. When finished, serve warm.

Per Serving: Calories 686; Fat 16.9g; Sodium 655mg; Carbs 8585g; Fiber 6.7g; Sugar 21.53g; Protein 47.43g

Savory Roasted Beef and Broccoli

⏰ Prep: 5 minutes　🍲 Cook: 10 minutes　🍃 Serves: 8

½ cup low-sodium soy sauce
4 to 5 cloves garlic, finely minced
2 to 3 tablespoons of honey
2 tablespoons packed brown sugar
2 tablespoons sesame oil
2 tablespoons rice vinegar
Optional
1 tablespoon cold water
1 tablespoon cornstarch
2 to 3 green onions, sliced in 1-inch segments

2 to 3 teaspoons of ground ginger
1 teaspoon kosher salt
1 teaspoon freshly ground black pepper
1-pound flank steak, sliced against the grain in bite-size pieces
4 to 6 cups of broccoli florets

on the bias (optional for garnishing)
1 tablespoon sesame seeds (optional for garnishing)

1. Mix the soy sauce, garlic, honey, brown sugar, sesame oil, rice vinegar, ginger, salt, and black pepper in a large bowl (you can also add the cayenne or red pepper flakes if you like). 2. Marinate the steak slices with the honey mixture for 10 to 15 minutes. 3. Transfer the marinated steak slices to the baking pan, leaving space between them. 4. Add the broccoli to the marinade bowl and give a quick dunk, then scatter them between the steak slices. 5. Reserve the marinade. 6. Roast the steak slices at 425°F/220°C for 12 minutes. 7. When done, evenly drizzle the dish with the reserved marinade. 8. You can garnish with green onions and sesame seeds before serving.

Per Serving: Calories 150; Fat 6.42g; Sodium 902mg; Carbs 8.82g; Fiber 0.8g; Sugar 6.47g; Protein 14.41g

Parsley-Crusted Pork Tenderloins

🕐 Prep: 15 minutes   🍲 Cook: 30 minutes   🥩 Serves: 6

2 pork tenderloins
1 cup soft bread crumbs
¼ cup chopped fresh parsley
½ teaspoon dried thyme leaves
1 tablespoon vegetable oil

½ teaspoon salt
½ teaspoon fennel seed
¼ teaspoon coarsely ground pepper
2 finely chopped cloves of garlic

1. Mix up all the ingredients except for the pork tenderloins in the bowl. 2. Place the pork tenderloins in the baking pan, and then spoon the herb mixture over them. 3. Loosely cover the pork tenderloins with the foil. 4. Bake the pork tenderloins at 450°F/230°C for 30 minutes. 5. After 20 minutes of cooking time, remove the foil and continue cooking. 6. Lightly cover the pork tenderloins again, and let them sit for 10 to 15 minutes before serving.

Per Serving: Calories 198; Fat 6.42g; Sodium 287mg; Carbs 3.58g; Fiber 0.4g; Sugar 0.36g; Protein 29.75g

Spiced Garlicky Lamb Skewers

🕐 Prep: 10 minutes   🍲 Cook: 10 minutes   🥩 Serves: 4

1-pound lamb shoulder chops, cut into 1-inch pieces
1 teaspoon fennel seed, crushed
1 tablespoon ground cumin
1 tablespoon red chili flakes, crushed

2 teaspoons dry sherry
1 tablespoon olive oil
2 teaspoons granulated garlic
1 teaspoon kosher salt

1. Mix the meat pieces with other ingredients in a large mixing bowl. 2. Cover the bowl and let the ingredients sit for 20 minutes. 3. Thread the marinated meat pieces on the skewer, and then place the skewers in the baking pan. 4. Air Fry the skewers at 340°F/170°C for 10 minutes, turning them halfway through. 5. Serve hot.

Per Serving: Calories 228; Fat 14.09g; Sodium 694mg; Carbs 2.12g; Fiber 0.5g; Sugar 0.56g; Protein 23.85g

Cheese Beef-Rice Stuffed Bell Peppers

🕐 Prep: 15 minutes   🍲 Cook: 15 minutes   🥩 Serves: 6

6 green bell peppers
1-pound lean ground beef
1 tablespoon olive oil
¼ cup green onion diced
¼ cup fresh parsley
½ teaspoon ground sage

½ teaspoon garlic salt
1 cup cooked rice
1 cup marinara sauce (more according to your taste)
¼ cup shredded Mozzarella cheese

1. Cook the ground beef in the skillet over medium to medium-high heat; drain the beef and return to the skillet. 2. Add the green onion, sage, parsley, salt, and olive oil to a large mixing bowl and mix well. 3. Add the cooked rice and marinara sauce and mix to combine thoroughly. Mix all the mixtures in a large mixing bowl. 4. Cut off the tops of the peppers and discard the seeds. 5. Fill in each pepper with the mixture and arrange the food on the cooking tray, then place the tray in the air fryer. 6. Bake the food at 355°F/179°C for 15 minutes. 7. When the cooking time is up, carefully remove the food from the air fryer. 8. Add the cheese on top and continue cooking for 5 minutes more until the peppers are softened, and the cheese has melted. 9. Serve and enjoy!

Per Serving: Calories 283; Fat 14.95g; Sodium 393mg; Carbs 17.55g; Fiber 5.8g; Sugar 4.39g; Protein 25.94g

Beef-Onion Skewers

⏰ Prep: 30 minutes   🍲 Cook: 10 minutes   🍃 Serves: 4

1-pound beef chuck ribs cut in 1-inch pieces or any other tender cut meat- think nice steak, stew meat
⅓ cup low-fat sour cream

2 tablespoons soy sauce
1 bell pepper, cut into 1-inch slices
½ onion, cut into 1-inch slices
8 6-inch skewers

1. Mix the sour cream and soy sauce in a medium bowl, then add the beef chunks to the bowl and marinate them for at least 30 minutes (it's better to marinate the beef chunks for overnight). 2. Soak the skewers in the water for 10 minutes. 3. Then thread the beef, bell peppers, and onions on the prepared skewers. 4. Season them with freshly ground black pepper. 5. Air Fry the skewers at 400°F/200°C for 10 minutes, turning them over halfway through cooking. 6. Carefully remove from the air fryer. 7. Serve and enjoy!

Per Serving: Calories 270; Fat 16.92g; Sodium 279mg; Carbs 5.52g; Fiber 0.3g; Sugar 3.31g; Protein 24.17g

Cajun Croutons-Crusted Pork Chops

⏰ Prep: 10 minutes   🍲 Cook: 10 minutes   🍃 Serves: 4

4 boneless, centre-cut pork chops, 1-inch thick
1 teaspoon Cajun seasoning
1 ½ cups cheese and garlic-flavoured croutons
2 eggs
Cooking spray

1. On a platter, rub the Cajun seasoning over the pork chops. 2. Blend the croutons in a small food processor and transfer them to a shallow plate. 3. Beat the eggs in a separate bowl and dip in the pork chops. Coat the pork chops with crouton breading. Then spray the coated pork chops with cooking spray. 4. Spray the cooking tray with cooking spray. 5. Arrange the pork chops evenly inside the cooking tray, and then insert the cooking tray inside the air fryer. 6. Air Fry the pork chops at 390°F/200°C for 10 minutes, flipping them and misting again halfway through cooking. 7. When the cooking time is up, carefully remove the food from the air fryer and transfer the food to a serving plate. 8. Serve and enjoy!

Per Serving: Calories 285; Fat 15.37g; Sodium 734mg; Carbs 1.84g; Fiber 0.1g; Sugar 1.11g; Protein 33.27g

Broiled Rib Eye Steak with Blue Cheese Butter

⏰ Prep: 15 minutes   🍲 Cook: 10 minutes   🍃 Serves: 4

32 ounces rib-eye steaks (two steaks) at least 1-inch-thick (12-16 ounces each)
2 teaspoons kosher salt
Blue Cheese Butter
4 ounces salted butter at room temperature

1.5 teaspoons freshly ground black pepper
1 teaspoon garlic powder

4 ounces blue cheese

To make the Blue Cheese Butter: 1. Mix the blue cheese and butter in a medium mixing bowl, mashing with a fork to incorporate them well. 2. Portion the mixture into seven servings and place one in each well. 3. Cover and freeze until ready to use, or harden in the refrigerator for 15 minutes and use right away.
For the Steak: 1. Defrost the rib-eye steak 15 minutes earlier before cooking. 2. Rub the salt, pepper, and garlic powder over both sides of the steaks. Press to season. 3. Arrange the steak onto the cooking tray, and place the tray in the air fryer. 4. Broil the steak at 400°F/200°C for 15 minutes, flipping after 4 minutes of cooking and continue cooking. 5. Power off the air fryer and allow the steak to stand in the air fryer uncovered for 1 minute for rare, 2 minutes for medium-rare, and 3 minutes for less rare. 6. Carefully remove the food from the air fryer and transfer to a serving plate. 7. Serve with the blue cheese butter, and enjoy!

Per Serving: Calories 898; Fat 78.71g; Sodium 1800mg; Carbs 1.8g; Fiber 0.3g; Sugar 0.18g; Protein 47.17g

Honey Pineapple-Flavored Ham

⏰ Prep: 10 minutes 🍲 Cook: 35 minutes 🍥 Serves: 12

3 pounds cooked ham, boneless
¼ teaspoon ground nutmeg
¼ teaspoon ground cinnamon
½ teaspoon cayenne
½ teaspoon smoked paprika

1 tablespoon honey
2 tablespoons apple cider vinegar
2 tablespoons pineapple juice
½ cup brown sugar
¼ teaspoon salt

1. Mix the brown sugar, pineapple juice, apple cider vinegar, cayenne pepper, nutmeg, cinnamon, salt, and paprika in a small bowl. Reserve half of the mixture. 2. Brush the unreserved mixture over the ham and cover with foil. 3. Place the ham in the baking pan, and then place the pan in the air fryer. 4. Bake the ham with the mixture at 320°F/160°C for 15 minutes. 5. When the cooking time is up, carefully remove the food from the air fryer and transfer the food to a cutting board. 6. Remove the foil and let it cool for several minutes. Then cut into your desired-sized ham slices. 7. Drizzle the slices with the reserved honey glaze. Serve and enjoy!

Per Serving: Calories 159; Fat 3.9g; Sodium 1502mg; Carbs 12.06g; Fiber 0.1g; Sugar 10.62g; Protein 19.22g

Spicy Lemony Steak Bites

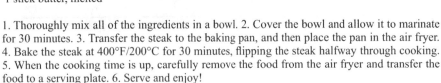

⏰ Prep: 10 minutes 🍲 Cook: 10 minutes 🍥 Serves: 6

1-pound rib-eye steak, cut into pieces
¼ teaspoon red pepper flakes
½ teaspoon garlic powder
1 tablespoon lemon juice
1 tablespoon lemon zest
1 stick butter, melted

1 tablespoon parsley, chopped
½ teaspoon Worcestershire sauce
½ tablespoon Dijon mustard
Pepper
Salt

1. Thoroughly mix all of the ingredients in a bowl. 2. Cover the bowl and allow it to marinate for 30 minutes. 3. Transfer the steak to the baking pan, and then place the pan in the air fryer. 4. Bake the steak at 400°F/200°C for 30 minutes, flipping the steak halfway through cooking. 5. When the cooking time is up, carefully remove the food from the air fryer and transfer the food to a serving plate. 6. Serve and enjoy!

Per Serving: Calories 337; Fat 31.2g; Sodium 210mg; Carbs 1.19g; Fiber 0.2g; Sugar 0.31g; Protein 13.91g

Garlicky Tri-Tip Steaks

⏰ Prep: 10 minutes 🍲 Cook: 12 minutes 🍥 Serves: 2

12 ounces tri-tip steak
1 teaspoon garlic, minced
2 tablespoons butter, melted

Pepper
Salt

1. Combine the butter, garlic, salt, and pepper in a small mixing bowl. 2. Rub the mixture over both sides of the steak and place in the baking pan, then place the pan in the air fryer. 3. Broil the steak at 400°F/200°C for 12 minutes, turning the steak to the other side halfway through cooking. 4. When the cooking time is up, carefully remove the food from the air fryer. 5. Transfer to a serving plate. Serve and enjoy!

Per Serving: Calories 558; Fat 37.38g; Sodium 292mg; Carbs 1.21g; Fiber 0.3g; Sugar 0.03g; Protein 51.31g

Chapter 7 Desserts Recipes

Homemade Leches Cake

⏰ Prep: 10 minutes   🍱 Cook: 60 minutes   🍽 Serves: 12

1 tablespoon unsalted butter
1 cup all-purpose flour
2 teaspoons baking powder
1 cup sugar
4 large egg whites
2 egg yolks
1 teaspoon vanilla extract

2 tablespoons + 2 teaspoons whole milk
⅔ cup coconut milk
⅔ cup evaporated milk
⅔ cup sweetened condensed milk
2 teaspoons coconut rum
Sweetened whipped cream

1. Whisk the baking powder and flour together in the bowl. 2. Beat the egg whites in a mixing bowl until the whites form soft peaks, and then gradually beat in the sugar. 3. Add the egg yolks one at a time and mix well. 4. Mix up the whole milk and vanilla in another bowl; add the flour mixture in 3 batches, alternating with milk in 2 batches, beginning and ending with the flour. 5. Butter the bottom and sides of the baking pan, and then pour the batter into the pan. 6. Bake the food at 350°F/175°C for 20 minutes. 7. When the time is up, adjust the cooking temperature to 325°F/160°C, and then resume baking the cake until golden brown and when you touch it, the center of the cake springs back. 8. Allow the cake to cool for 15 minutes on the wire rack. 9. In a medium bowl, whisk the evaporated milk, sweetened condensed milk, coconut milk, and the rum well. 10. Poke holes all over the top of the cake with a skewer and let the liquid absorb before adding more. 11. Garnish the cake with whipped cream.

Per Serving: Calories 175; Fat 7.32g; Sodium 57mg; Carbs 22.98g; Fiber 0.6g; Sugar 14.17g; Protein 4.88g

Cinnamon Apple Chips

⏰ Prep: 10 minutes   🍱 Cook: 10 minutes   🍽 Serves: 4

2 apples, cored and sliced
2 heaped teaspoons of ground cinnamon

Cooking spray

1. Grease the cooking tray with the cooking spray. 2. Coat the apple slices with the cinnamon and then place them on the tray. 3. Air Fry the apple slices at 350°F/175°C for 10 minutes until they are crisp, stirring them halfway through cooking. 4. Let the apple chips rest for 5 minutes before serving.

Per Serving: Calories 51; Fat 0.17g; Sodium 1mg; Carbs 13.61g; Fiber 2.9g; Sugar 9.48g; Protein 0.29g

Cream Cheese Chocolate Mug Cake

⏰ Prep: 10 minutes   🍱 Cook: 15 minutes   🍽 Serves: 3

½ cup of cocoa powder
½ cup stevia powder
1 cup coconut cream
One package of cream cheese, room

temperature
1 tablespoon vanilla extract
1 tablespoon butter

1. Mix up all the ingredients in a mixing bowl. 2. Use a hand mixer to blend the whole thing until fluffy, then apportion the mixture between the greased mugs. 3. Place the mugs in the cooking tray. 4. Bake the mugs at 350°F/185°C for 15 minutes. 5. Chill the cakes in the fridge before serving.

Per Serving: Calories 388; Fat 36.77g; Sodium 61mg; Carbs 22.76g; Fiber 10.3g; Sugar 1.23g; Protein 8.49g

Tasty Oat-Berries Crisp

⏱ **Prep: 20 minutes** 🍴 **Cook: 35 minutes** 🍽 **Serves: 7**

¾ cup all-purpose flour
½ cup old fashioned rolled oats
½ cup packed light brown sugar
¼ cup granulated sugar
¼ teaspoon cinnamon
¼ teaspoon salt
½ cup unsalted butter, cold, diced into small

pieces
Filling
12 ounces of fresh raspberries
11 ounces of fresh blueberries
6 ounces fresh blackberries
⅓ cup granulated sugar
1½ tablespoon cornstarch

To make the crumble: 1. Mix up all the crumble ingredients except the butter in a mixing bowl. 2. Add the butter and cut into the mixture with a pastry cutter until the mixture resembles coarse crumbs. 3. Transfer the bowl to the refrigerator.
To make the filling: 1. Butter the baking pan. 2. Rinse and drain the berries. Transfer them to the baking pan. 3. Mix up the sugar and cornstarch in a bowl, then coat the berries with the mixture. 4. Remove the crumble from the refrigerator and sprinkle evenly over the berries. 5. Bake the food at 375°F/190°C for 35 minutes until the filling are bubbling and the topping is golden brown and crisp. 6. Serve warm.

Per Serving: Calories 279; Fat 10.28g; Sodium 97mg; Carbs 46.87g; Fiber 6.2g; Sugar 24.61g; Protein 4.47g

Air Fried Pecan Pie

⏱ **Prep: 10 minutes** 🍴 **Cook: 35 minutes** 🍽 **Serves: 5**

¾ cup brown sugar
¼ cup caster sugar
⅓ cup butter, melted
4 large eggs
1¾ tablespoons flour

1 tablespoon milk
1 teaspoon vanilla extract
1 cup pecan halves
1 frozen pie crust, thawed

1. Mix up the sugars, butter, and eggs in a large bowl until foamy. 2. Mix the foamy mixture with the flour, milk, and vanilla extract until well combined. 3. Fold in the pecan halves. 4. Grease the baking pan and transfer the crust to the pan. 5. Arrange the crust on the bottom of the prepared baking pan, then evenly place the pecan mixture over the crust. 6. Arrange the pan in the air fryer. 7. Air Fry the pie at 300°F/150°C for 22 minutes. 8. When the time is up, reset the cooking temperature to 120°F/50°C and the timer to 10 minutes. 9. Place the pie pan onto a wire rack to cool for about 20 minutes before serving.

Per Serving: Calories 597; Fat 39.08g; Sodium 334mg; Carbs 55.3g; Fiber 2.2g; Sugar 38.13g; Protein 9.1g

The Best Blueberry Pie

⏱ **Prep: 10 minutes** 🍴 **Cook: 50 minutes** 🍽 **Serves: 4**

Store-bought pie crust dough
6 cups fresh blueberries
⅔ cup granulated sugar
¼ cup cornstarch
¼ teaspoon ground cinnamon
1 tablespoon lemon juice

1 tablespoon unsalted butter, cut into small pieces
1 large egg, lightly beaten with 1 tablespoon of milk
Coarse sugar for garnish (optional)

Make the filling: 1. Mix the blueberries with granulated sugar, cinnamon, cornstarch, and lemon juice in a large mixing bowl. 2. Sprinkle enough flour on a work surface and roll out one of the discs of chilled dough. Turn the dough a quarter of a turn every few rolls until it is a 12-inch circle. in diameter. 3. Carefully flatten the dough in the pie dish. 4. Spoon the filling into the crust, leaving any excess liquid in the bowl; top the filling with the butter slices.
Arrange the lattice: 1. Roll the other disc of chilled pie dough into a circle that's 12 inches in diameter. 2. Cut 1- to 2-inch-wide strips with a sharp knife; carefully thread the strips over and under one another, pulling strips back to weave as necessary. 3. Press the edges of the strips into the bottom pie crust edges to seal. Use a small knife to trim off excess dough. Crimp the edges with a fork as needed. 4. Lightly brush the top of the pie crust with the egg-milk mixture; sprinkle the top with a little coarse sugar (optional). 5. Arrange the pie to a suitable baking sheet. 6. Bake the pie at 400°F/200°C for 20 minutes. 7. When the time is up, keep the pie in the air fryer, turn the temperature down to 350°F/175°C and bake it for 25 to 30 minutes. 8. After 20 minutes of baking time, place a pie crust shield over the top of the pie to prevent the edges from browning too quickly. 9. Allow the pie to cool for 3 hours at oat temperature before serving.

Per Serving: Calories 459; Fat 16.03g; Sodium 314mg; Carbs 76.84g; Fiber 6.2g; Sugar 38.64g; Protein 6.05g

Fluffy Cinnamon Cakes

⏰ **Prep:** 15 minutes   🍲 **Cook:** 55 minutes   🍃 **Serves:** 12

For the cinnamon filling
¾ cup light brown sugar
¼ cup all-purpose flour
2 teaspoons ground cinnamon
For the streusel
⅔ cup light brown sugar, lightly packed
For the cake
2¼ cup all-purpose flour
¼ cup cornstarch
2½ teaspoons baking powder
¾ teaspoon salt
¾ cup unsalted butter

1 cup all-purpose flour
2 teaspoons ground cinnamon
¼ teaspoon salt
½ cup unsalted butter, diced

½ cup brown sugar
1 cup granulated sugar
3 large eggs (room temperature)
2 teaspoons extract
1 cup sour cream

To make the cinnamon filling: 1. Mix up the brown sugar, flour, and cinnamon in a bowl and then set aside.
To make the streusel topping: 1. Whisk the brown sugar, salt, cinnamon, and flour in another bowl, then add the diced butter. 2. Press and crumble the butter into the dry mixture, and set aside for later use. (For larger crumbles, try pressing a large handful together and break apart into large pieces.)
To make the cake: 1. Whisk the flour, cornstarch, baking powder, and salt in the third bowl and then set aside. 2. Beat the butter and granulated sugar in a stand mixer fitted with a paddle attachment until light and fluffy, then add the brown sugar and mix on high speed. 3. Pour in the vanilla, then beat in the eggs one at a time while mixing on low. Scrape the bowl down, add the sour cream, and mix until combined. 4. Add the dry mixture to the wet and mix until just combined, then use a spatula to scrape the bowl down and mix in any stray bits. 5. Line the baking pan with parchment paper, pour half of the cake batter into the pan and smooth out, top the batter with the cinnamon filling and spread the batter with the remaining batter from the center to the edges; lastly, top the batter with the streusel. 6. Bake them at 350°F/175°C for 55 minutes. 7. When done, the toothpick inserted in the center should come out clean. 8. Allow the cake to cool in the pan for 20 minutes before cutting.

Per Serving: Calories 400; Fat 16.71g; Sodium 229mg; Carbs 56.84g; Fiber 1.5g; Sugar 23.05g; Protein 6.1g

Homemade Coco Almond Cake

⏰ **Prep:** 5 minutes   🍲 **Cook:** 10 minutes   🍃 **Serves:** 4

¼ cup all-purpose flour
3 tablespoons sugar
2 tablespoons cocoa powder
⅛ teaspoon baking soda
3 tablespoons almond milk
2 tablespoons olive oil

1 tablespoon warm water
2 drops vanilla extract (optional)
Pinch of salt
4 raw almonds, thinly chopped, for decoration (optional)

1. Mix up the milk, oil, water, and sugar in a medium bowl until a smooth batter formed. 2. Add the baking soda, all-purpose flour, salt, and cocoa powder to the milk bowl and whisk to form a smooth paste. 3. Oil a suitable cake pan and then pour the batter into it; top the batter with the chopped almonds (optional). 4. Tightly cover the pan with foil and place it in the air fryer. 5. Bake the cake at 350°F/175°C for 10 minutes. 6. When done, serve and enjoy.

Per Serving: Calories 124; Fat 7.55g; Sodium 86mg; Carbs 14.07g; Fiber 1g; Sugar 6.51g; Protein 1.65g

Cinnamon Peaches

⏰ **Prep:** 10 minutes   🍲 **Cook:** 15 minutes   🍃 **Serves:** 4

2 tablespoons sugar
¼ teaspoon ground cinnamon

4 peaches, each cut in half
Cooking spray

1. Evenly coat the peaches with sugar and cinnamon. 2. Lightly spray the cooking tray with cooking spray. 3. Place the peaches in the cooking tray in a single layer and lightly mist the peaches with cooking spray. 4. Air Fry the peaches at 350°F/175°C for 10 minutes, flipping them halfway through the cooking. 5. Let the peaches cool before serving.

Per Serving: Calories 89; Fat 0.1g; Sodium 6mg; Carbs 23.67g; Fiber 1.4g; Sugar 22.18g; Protein 0.45g

Flavorful Cinnamon Pecan Pie

🕐 **Prep: 2 hours 30 minutes**　🍲 **Cook: 55 minutes**　🍃 **Serves: 8**

Crust

1 pie crust dough, chilled
Egg wash for pie crust: 1 large egg beaten

with 1 tablespoon milk or heavy cream

Filling

2½ cups shelled pecans
3 large eggs
1 cup dark corn syrup
½ cup packed light or dark brown sugar
1½ teaspoon pure vanilla extract

¼ cup unsalted butter, melted and slightly
cooled
½ teaspoon salt
½ teaspoon ground cinnamon

Crust: 1. Preheat the air fryer to 350°F/175°C on Bake mode. 2. Sprinkle enough flour on the work surface, and roll the chilled pie crust out into a circle 12 inches in diameter on the work surface. 3. Carefully place the dough in a suitable pie dish and tuck it in with your fingers, making sure the dough is smooth. 4. Fold the overhanging dough back over the edges and use your hands to shape the edges into a nice thick rim around the pie. 5. Heartily place the dough into a suitable pie plate and tuck it in with your fingers, making sure the dough is smooth. 4. 4. Fold the overhanging dough back over the edges and use your hands to shape the edges into the thick sides of the pie. 5. Flatten the edges with a fork so that the edges are fluted. 6. Brush the edges with the egg wash.

To make the filling: 1. Very roughly chop the pecans, leaving some whole and some lightly chopped. Spread the pecans evenly inside the pie crust. 2. Thoroughly mix the eggs, corn syrup, brown sugar, vanilla, melted butter, salt, and cinnamon in a large bowl until combined.
3. Pour the egg mixture over the pecans. 4. Bake the pie at 350°F/175°C for 55 minutes. 5. When done, the top should be lightly browned. If the pie is browning too quickly, cover the entire pie with aluminum foil. 6. Remove the finished pie from the air fryer and place it onto a wire rack to cool completely. The pie filling will settle as it cools. 7. Cover and store leftovers at room temperature for up to 2 days or in the refrigerator for up to 5 days.

Per Serving: Calories 614; Fat 39.98g; Sodium 506mg; Carbs g; Fiber 62.59g; Sugar 39.29g; Protein 6.77g

Homemade Streusel Cake

🕐 **Prep: 10 minutes**　🍲 **Cook: 45 minutes**　🍃 **Serves: 8**

Streusel:

1½ cups firmly packed brown sugar
½ cup rolled oats

1 teaspoon cinnamon
2 tablespoons butter, chilled

Cake batter:

1½ cups all-purpose flour
1 teaspoon baking powder
1 teaspoon baking soda
¼ teaspoon nutmeg
½ teaspoon salt
6 tablespoons butter, softened

¾ cups sugar
2 eggs
1 teaspoon vanilla extract
¾ cup plain yogurt
½ cup apple butter

1. Mix up the brown sugar, oats, and two tablespoons of chilled butter to make the streusel in a suitable bowl. 2. Cream the softened butter and sugar in a mixer until smooth; beat in one egg at a time to the oats and sugar mixture; add the vanilla and the yogurt. 3. Whisk the dry ingredients together in another bowl. Once combined, fold the dry ingredients into the wet mixture. 4. Alternate the batter, apple butter, and streusel in a loaf pan. 5. Bake the food at 325°F/165°C for 45 minutes. 6. When done, the toothpick inserted into the center of the cake should come out clean.

Per Serving: Calories 446; Fat 18.77g; Sodium 495mg; Carbs 59.5g; Fiber 2g; Sugar 35.26g; Protein 12.07g

Vanilla Blueberry Pie

🕐 **Prep: 15 minutes**　🍲 **Cook: 45 minutes**　🍃 **Serves: 6**

5 cups blueberries
1-¼ cups granulated sugar
½ teaspoon lemon zest
1 pinch mace

2½ tablespoons cornstarch
3 tablespoons water
¾ teaspoon vanilla extract
2 sheets of store-bought pie dough

1. Whisk the cornstarch and water in a bowl. 2. Cook the blueberries, sugar, lemon zest, and mace in a small saucepan over medium heat for about 5 minutes or until the sugar has dissolved and the mixture begins to look soupy. 3. Pour in the cornstarch mixture and stir until the mixture begins to thicken. 4. Remove the saucepan from the heat and set aside to let the mixture cool. 5. Lightly flour the work surface, and roll out the dough sheets. 6. Place a pie pan on one of the dough sheets. Cut ¾-inch larger around the pan. 7. Press the dough into the pan, trim any excess dough from around the sides, and then add the filling. 8. To make the lattice top, cut the second sheet of dough into eight 1-inch pieces and weave the dough to form the lattice. 9. Transfer the lattice to the top of the pie. 10. Bake the pie at 310°F/155°C for 45 minutes. 11. Let the pie rest for about 2 hours before serving.

Per Serving: Calories 461; Fat 19.44g; Sodium 314mg; Carbs 70.25g; Fiber 4g; Sugar 22.63g; Protein 3.19g

Typical Cinnamon Churros

⏰ Prep: 10 minutes   🍲 Cook: 10 minutes   🍃 Serves: 4-6

4 tablespoons butter	2 large eggs
¼ teaspoon salt	2 teaspoons ground cinnamon
½ cup water	¼ cup granulated white sugar
½ cup all-purpose flour	Cooking spray

1. In the saucepan over high heat, add the butter, salt, and water, and bring them to a boil until the butter is melted. Keep stirring. 2. Lower the heat to medium and fold in the flour to form a dough. 3. Keep cooking and stirring until the dough is dried out; coat the pan with a crust. 4. Turn off the heat, transfer the dough to a large bowl, and let the dough cool for about 15 minutes. 5. Crack the eggs into the dough and mix them with a hand mixer until the dough is sanity and firm enough to shape. 6. Scoop up one tablespoon of the dough and roll it into a ½-inch-diameter and 2-inch long cylinder. Do the same with the remaining dough to make 12 cylinders in total. 7. In a large bowl, mix up the cinnamon and sugar and dip the cylinders into the cinnamon mix to coat. 8. Arrange the cylinders on a plate and refrigerate for 20 minutes. 9. Grease the cooking tray with cooking spray and place the cylinders in the cooking tray, and spritz with cooking spray. 10. Air Fry the churros at 375°F/190°C for 10 minutes, flipping them after 5 minutes of cooking time. 11. When cooked, the churros should be golden brown and fluffy. 12. Serve immediately.

Per Serving: Calories 145; Fat 10.9g; Sodium 162mg; Carbs 9.91g; Fiber 1g; Sugar 0.91g; Protein 2.33g

Mini Molten Chocolate Cakes

⏰ Prep: 5 minutes   🍲 Cook: 20 minutes   🍃 Serves: 6

¼ cup heavy cream	2 large eggs, separated, divided
8 ounces semi-sweet chocolate, chopped, divided	½ teaspoon vanilla extract
5 tablespoons unsalted butter, divided	1 pinch salt
5 tablespoons sugar, divided	3 tablespoons all-purpose flour

To make the ganache: 1. Bring the cream to simmer in the saucepan over low heat. 2. In a bowl, add 2 ounces of the chocolate and then pour the cream over the chocolate; stir them for 2 to 3 minutes to combine. 3. Chill the mixture until firm. 4. Form the mixture into six 1-inch balls. Store the ganache in the refrigerator.
To make the cakes: 1. Grease six 6-ounce ramekins with one teaspoon of butter in each ramekin; pour one teaspoon of sugar into each ramekin, turn to coat, and tap out any excess sugar. 2. Melt the remaining chocolate and add it to a bowl with four tablespoons of butter. Set the bowl over simmering water and stir to combine. 3. Allow the chocolate to cool slightly, and then stir in the vanilla, egg yolks, and flour. 4. Whip the egg whites in the electric mixer until thickened and foamy. 5. Gradually beat in 3 tablespoons of sugar and continue beating until stiff peaks form. 6. Fold the egg whites into the chocolate mixture and combine them well. 7. Evenly divide the batter between the prepared ramekins. Press a ganache ball into each ramekin and cover with the batter. 8. Bake the cakes at 325°F/165°C for 15 minutes. 9. Let the cakes cool for 3 minutes after baking. Serve and enjoy.

Per Serving: Calories 326; Fat 22.75g; Sodium 41mg; Carbs 32.85g; Fiber 2.2g; Sugar 26.21g; Protein 3.26g

Apple Dumplings

⏰ Prep: 10 minutes   🍲 Cook: 25 minutes   🍃 Serves: 4

2 tablespoons melted coconut oil	2 tablespoons raisins
2 puff pastry sheets, cut into the size desired	2 small apples
1 tablespoon brown sugar	

1. Core and peel apples and mix with raisins and sugar. 2. Place a bit of apple mixture on the middle of puff pastry sheets and brush the sides with melted coconut oil to knead the pastry. 3. Arrange the apple dumplings in the baking pan. 4. Bake the dumplings at 355°F/180°C for 25 minutes until they are golden on the surface, turning them over halfway through cooking. 5. You can serve them with vanilla ice cream.

Per Serving: Calories 235; Fat 15.88g; Sodium 59mg; Carbs 23.08g; Fiber 2.1g; Sugar 10.02g; Protein 1.92g

Baked Walnut Pie

⏰ Prep: 5 minutes 🍲 Cook: 35 minutes 🍽 Serves: 6

All-purpose flour for dusting
1 store-bought or homemade prepared pie dough, room temperature
1½ cups walnuts, chopped
4 large eggs

1⅓ cups light corn syrup
⅔ cup light brown sugar
2 tablespoons unsalted butter, melted
1¼ teaspoons vanilla extract
½ teaspoon salt

1. Lightly dust a work surface with the flour and roll out the pie dough. 2. Fold the edges of the dough under itself so that the folded edges are above the rim of your pie pan. Curl the edges of the pie dough to form a decorative edge. 3. Place the walnuts in the pie shell. 4. Mix up the eggs, corn syrup, brown sugar, melted butter, vanilla, and salt in a bowl until smooth. 5. Pour the mixture over the nuts in the pie shell, then place it in the air fryer. 6. Bake the pie at 300°F/150°C for 35 minutes. 7. When done, the crust should be golden brown, and the pie should be just set. 8. Let the pie cool for at least 50 minutes before serving.

Per Serving: Calories 587; Fat 28.81g; Sodium 411mg; Carbs 82,24g; Fiber 1.8g; Sugar 59.21g; Protein 6.43g

Strawberry Oats Crumble

⏰ Prep: 15 minutes 🍲 Cook: 35 minutes 🍽 Serves: 6

6 cups strawberries
1 tablespoon fresh lemon juice
2 tablespoons all-purpose flour
3 tablespoons light brown sugar, divided
⅓ cup almond flour
⅓ cup rolled oats

½ teaspoon baking powder
½ teaspoon cinnamon
⅛ teaspoon salt
3 tablespoons cold unsalted butter, cut into pieces

1. Lightly grease the baking pan with cooking spray. 2. Arrange the strawberries on the bottom of the pan and toss them with lemon juice. 3. Combine the flour and one tablespoon of light brown sugar in a small bowl until incorporated. 4. Add the brown sugar mixture to the strawberries and mix to combine. Set aside. 5. Mix up the almond flour, oats, baking powder, cinnamon, salt, and the remaining brown sugar in the mixing bowl. 6. Rub in the butter until the mixture is crumbly. 7. Press the mixture between your fingers into small lumps and sprinkle over the strawberries. 8. Bake the food at 375°F/190°C for 35 minutes until the top is golden brown and the fruit is bubbling. 9. Remove the food from the air fryer and let stand for a few minutes.

Per Serving: Calories 111; Fat 4.72g; Sodium 57mg; Carbs 18.5g; Fiber 3.9g; Sugar 8.65g; Protein 2.39g

Hazelnuts Orange Cake

⏰ Prep: 10 minutes 🍲 Cook: 20 minutes 🍽 Serves: 6

1 stick of butter, at room temperature
5 tablespoons liquid monk fruit
2 eggs plus one egg yolk, beaten
⅓ cup hazelnuts, roughly chopped
3 tablespoons sugar-free orange marmalade
6 ounces almond flour

1 teaspoon baking soda
½ teaspoon baking powder
½ teaspoon ground cinnamon
½ teaspoon ground allspice
½ teaspoon ground anise seed
Cooking spray

1. Lightly spritz the baking pan with cooking spray. 2. Mix up the butter and liquid monk fruit in a bowl until the mixture is pale and smooth. 3. Mix in the beaten eggs, hazelnuts, and marmalade and whisk again until well incorporated. 4. Add the almond flour, baking soda, baking powder, cinnamon, allspice, and anise seed and mix well. 5. Transfer the batter to the baking pan. 6. Bake the cake at 310°F/155°C for 20 minutes. 7. When finished, gently press the top of the cake with your finger; the cake should spring back. 8. Transfer the cake to a wire rack and let the cake cool to room temperature before serving.

Per Serving: Calories 474; Fat 44.66g; Sodium 335mg; Carbs 14.15g; Fiber 6.1g; Sugar 5.3g; Protein 10.54g

Soft Chocolate Lava Cakes

🕐 **Prep: 10 minutes**　🍲 **Cook: 15 minutes**　🍃 **Serves: 6**

6 ounces semi-sweet chocolate
½ cup unsalted butter
¼ cup all-purpose flour
½ cup confectioners' sugar

⅛ teaspoon salt
2 large eggs
2 large egg yolks

1. Spray four muffin cups with nonstick cooking spray and dust with cocoa powder. Set aside. 2. Coarsely chop the chocolate. 3. Add the butter to a medium heat-proof bowl, and then top the butter with the chopped chocolate. 4. Place the butter-chocolate bowl in the microwave and heat on high in 10-second increments, stirring after each heat, until completely smooth. Set aside. 5. Mix up the flour, confectioners' sugar, and salt in a small bowl. In another bowl, whisk the eggs and egg yolks together until combined. 6. Pour the flour mixture and eggs into the bowl of chocolate, and slowly stir everything together. The batter will be slightly thick. 7. Spoon the chocolate batter evenly into each prepared muffin cup and then arrange the cups in the baking pan. 8. Bake them at 425°F/220°C in the air fryer for 15 minutes. 9. The sides should appear solid and firm when done—the tops will still look soft. 10. Allow the cakes to cool for 1 minute, then cover each with an inverted plate and carefully turn over.

Per Serving: Calories 325; Fat 23.04g; Sodium 69mg; Carbs 29.83g; Fiber 1.7g; Sugar 22.82g; Protein 4.06g

Conclusion

The air fryer functions like a compact convection oven, circulating hot air around the food, which means it needs far less oil than traditional frying methods. This leads to uniformly cooked, crispy results, perfect for dishes like French fries and chicken wings. Air frying not only offers a healthier alternative to deep frying but can also cut down on cooking time. When using an air fryer, it's important to avoid overfilling the basket to prevent uneven cooking. Make sure to shake or flip the food midway through the cooking process for consistent browning. Additionally, keep a close watch on your food as air fryers tend to cook rapidly and sometimes unpredictably. With these pointers, you're on your way to mastering air frying.

Air fryers are a fantastic and healthy option for cooking food with minimal oil. They help you steer clear of unhealthy fats and provide a speedy, convenient cooking method for busy households. If you're in search of a healthy, easy cooking solution or just a faster way to prepare dinner, consider getting an air fryer.

If you haven't bought one yet, now is the perfect time. An air fryer is a wonderful tool to broaden your cooking skills, simplify meal preparation, and enjoy your favorite fried dishes without the guilt. With an air fryer, there's ample opportunity for experimentation and tailoring dishes to your taste preferences at every meal. Check out the diverse range of air fryers available today!

Appendix 1 Measurement Conversion Chart

VOLUME EQUIVALENTS (LIQUID)

US STANDARD	US STANDARD (OUNCES)	METRIC (APPROXIMATE)
2 tablespoons	1 fl.oz	30 mL
¼ cup	2 fl.oz	60 mL
½ cup	4 fl.oz	120 mL
1 cup	8 fl.oz	240 mL
1½ cup	12 fl.oz	355 mL
2 cups or 1 pint	16 fl.oz	475 mL
4 cups or 1 quart	32 fl.oz	1 L
1 gallon	128 fl.oz	4 L

VOLUME EQUIVALENTS (DRY)

US STANDARD	METRIC (APPROXIMATE)
⅛ teaspoon	0.5 mL
¼ teaspoon	1 mL
½ teaspoon	2 mL
¾ teaspoon	4 mL
1 teaspoon	5 mL
1 tablespoon	15 mL
¼ cup	59 mL
½ cup	118 mL
¾ cup	177 mL
1 cup	235 mL
2 cups	475 mL
3 cups	700 mL
4 cups	1 L

TEMPERATURES EQUIVALENTS

FAHRENHEIT (F)	CELSIUS (C) (APPROXIMATE)
225°F	107°C
250°F	120°C
275°F	135°C
300°F	150°C
325°F	160°C
350°F	180°C
375°F	190°C
400°F	205°C
425°F	220°C
450°F	235°C
475°F	245°C
500°F	260°C

WEIGHT EQUIVALENTS

US STANDARD	METRIC (APPROXINATE)
1 ounce	28 g
2 ounces	57 g
5 ounces	142 g
10 ounces	284 g
15 ounces	425g
16 ounces (1 pound)	455 g
1.5pounds	680 g
2pounds	907g

Appendix 2 Air Fryer Cooking Chart

Meat and Seafood	Temp (°F)	Time (min)	Vegetables	Temp (°F)	Time (min)
Bacon	400	5 to 10	Asparagus	375	4 to 6
Beef Eye Round Roast (4 lbs.)	390	45 to 55	Baked Potatoes	400	35 to 45
Bone to in Pork Chops	400	4 to 5 per side	Broccoli	400	8 to 10
Brats	400	8 to 10	Brussels Sprouts	350	15 to 18
Burgers	350	8 to 10	Butternut Squash (cubed)	375	20 to 25
Chicken Breast	375	22 to 23	Carrots	375	15 to 25
Chicken Tender	400	14 to 16	Cauliflower	400	10 to 12
Chicken Thigh	400	25	Corn on the Cob	390	6
Chicken Wings (2 lbs.)	400	10 to 12	Eggplant	400	15
Cod	370	8 to 10	Green Beans	375	16 to 20
Fillet Mignon (8 oz.)	400	14 to 18	Kale	250	12
Fish Fillet (0.5 lb., 1-inch)	400	10	Mushrooms	400	5
Flank Steak(1.5 lbs.)	400	10 to 14	Peppers	375	8 to 10
Lobster Tails (4 oz.)	380	5 to 7	Sweet Potatoes (whole)	380	30 to 35
Meatballs	400	7 to 10	Tomatoes (halved, sliced)	350	10
Meat Loaf	325	35 to 45	Zucchini (½-inch sticks)	400	12
Pork Chops	375	12 to 15			
Salmon	400	5 to 7			
Salmon Fillet (6 oz.)	380	12	Frozen Foods	Temp (°F)	Time (min)
Sausage Patties	400	8 to 10	Breaded Shrimp	400	9
Shrimp	375	8	Chicken Burger	360	11
Steak	400	7 to 14	Chicken Nudgets	400	10
Tilapia	400	8 to 12	Corn Dogs	400	7
Turkey Breast (3 lbs.)	360	40 to 50	Curly Fries (1 to 2 lbs.)	400	11 to 14
Whole Chicken (6.5 lbs.)	360	75	Fish Sticks (10 oz.)	400	10
			French Fries	380	15 to 20
Desserts	Temp (°F)	Time (min)	Hash Brown	360	15 to 18
Apple Pie	320	30	Meatballs	380	6 to 8
Brownies	350	17	Mozzarella Sticks	400	8
Churros	360	13	Onion Rings (8 oz.)	400	8
Cookies	350	5	Pizza	390	5 to 10
Cupcakes	330	11	Pot Pie	360	25
Doughnuts	360	5	Pot Sticks (10 oz.)	400	8
Roasted Bananas	375	8	Sausage Rolls	400	15
Peaches	350	5	Spring Rolls	400	15 to 20

Appendix 3 Recipes Index

Made in the USA
Monee, IL
20 December 2024

74968807R00044